REQUIE...
PA...

by Rev.

A church with a crepe on the door — such an image might be suggested by the title, *Requiem for a Parish*. This, however, is not the author's intention. But although Father Foster does not contend that parish life is dead, he does believe that it is in a rut.

The Christian formation of many Catholics has been too superficial. They attend Mass regularly, receive the sacraments frequently, insist on a Catholic education for their children, strongly oppose divorce — yet when demands, outside of normal parish procedure, are made upon their faith and charity, these Catholics display a spiritual destitution.

Why is this? Father Foster suggests that this condition may be a result of over-organization of Christian life in the parish. Where there is too much concern for the organized life of the Church, the organic life of a parish may be gradually stifled out of existence.

Basing his work firmly on the Church's teaching, with many references to recent encyclicals, Father Foster has produced a detailed inquiry into customary practice and procedure in the contemporary parish that is critical, constructive, and controversial.

· *Requiem for a Parish* ·

· *Requiem for a Parish* ·

an inquiry into customary practices and
procedures in the contemporary parish

by John Foster

The Newman Press, Westminster, Maryland

• *1963* •

First published 1962
Second printing 1963

Library of Congress Catalog Card Number: 62–16214 7/11/74

Nihil obstat: Edward A. Cerny, S.S., S.T.D.
Censor librorum

Imprimatur: ✠ Francis P. Keough, D.D.
Archbishop of Baltimore

July 24, 1961

Contents

Foreword

My title suggests a lament. But the intention is otherwise. Far from believing that the parish as we know it is dead, one can identify within it certain stirrings of new life. And since in all times, as Cardinal Newman wrote, the laity have been the measure of the Catholic spirit, we cannot go far wrong if we link present and future development of parish life with the arrival on the contemporary scene of a new type of Catholic laity being formed in the Church for a new age, a laity with a greater spiritual maturity, stronger and surer of itself in the world, closer to God in its sense of mystery. Requiem, yes, but in the traditional sense, as the reward for past efforts and labor in tilling the ungrateful ground of modern industrialized urban society. *In labore requies.* Far from having had its day, the day for a full flowering of parish life has still to come. All the more important, therefore, that we recognize the stirrings of new life for what they really are, emphasize the creative possibilities open to the parish community, follow the right signposts, and not deep-freeze the present situation within the limited ambitions of the past. Requiem for a parish will thus be seen, not as a resting on laurels won in past endeavors, but as the prelude to a future of renewed activity and vigor.

I am grateful to the Editor of *The Clergy Review* for permission to reprint sections of the chapters on "Missionary Method in a Parish" and "Lay Spirituality."

J. F.

· *Requiem for a Parish* ·

A Plum of a Parish

*We are hiding corruption and
throwing a veil over putrefaction.*
ERIK PETERSON in
A Theology of Clothes

A "plum of a parish" is clerical jargon for the kind of well-established, financially secure, and solid parish with which a member of the diocesan clergy could expect to be rewarded after long service in the diocesan vineyard. There are certain proprieties to be preserved even in the matter of clerical appointments. If, as a priest, you have notched up many victories over local educational authorities in the matter of church schools, then to allow you to remain in one of those *parvenu* parishes in the outer suburbs would be slightly incongruous: in any case, a man of your ability should be more, as it were, on the doorstep of the diocesan headquarters. Equally unfitting would it be to send the late rector of the diocesan seminary to a small place in a newly-built area, with the deed to half an acre of ground, and tell him to build rectory, church, and school with nothing more than a blessing. A ~~priest with such renown~~ needs, deserves, a parish with an air of distinction, with a little history ~~behind~~ it. This would be the so-called "plum of a parish."

Though you may not approve of the architecture or furnishings of the church, there is little else you could find fault with in such a parish. It looks well-cared for; services are always punctual; people are continually dropping into the church during the day to pay visits to the Blessed Sacrament; at night, the rectory is a blaze of light; on Saturdays, wedding parties in the mornings and afternoons, queues outside the confessional boxes in the evening; on Sundays, cars in abundance outside, not only of parishioners, but of those from adjoining parishes who prefer the tone of this.

Such a parish is visited regularly by the clergy who are frequently invited to dinner. There are plenty of societies and organizations catering for every taste and need. The school has a loyal staff whose members leave only to get married. Boy Scouts and Girl Guides of the superior type add color and prestige to any celebration.

Nothing is said of the number of Communion hosts consecrated each week, of the sales of Catholic newspapers, of the boxes of votive candles, of the big Whitsun reception of converts, of the tennis club, of the outdoor crib, of the local Catholic town councilors, of the choir and servers' guild: one can well imagine how favorably all these compare with any others in the diocese.

On one such "plum of a parish," a bomb fell one day in the shape of twenty young Hungarians. It was during the recent rebellion in Hungary. They arrived early one morning and were lodged in a derelict building once used as the workhouse. It was, it appeared to be, a foregone conclusion that within a matter of hours these Hungarian boys would be whisked away from the coldness of the reception center to the warmth of twenty welcoming Catholic families.

Surprisingly, nothing of the kind happened. The boys remained in the workhouse, proved very difficult, and inflicted certain damages on the local lads: revolutionaries who had fought for a cause were new to them.

Today those Hungarian boys are no longer in the parish. They arrived, and they departed; and are now forgotten. But while they were here, deep down in the life of this "plum of a parish," something had stirred. It was an almost imperceptible movement, but it caused the perspicacious a certain alarm. Had the foundations shifted? Were there cracks in the structure of the building? Had the cornerstone slipped?

Such misgivings fed themselves on recent memories of other disquiet. There was the day when the university chaplain had appealed at every Mass for hospitality for the foreign students lodging in the parish. Some of the parishioners had already a kind of proprietary interest in these students, for some, as "black babies," had received at baptism the names of their sponsors. Strange that, in this case, the child had not become the father of the man, that the now adult Christians of the parish had lost all interest in their former spiritual offspring. "Black babies," yes, but full-grown African students, no. The chaplain departed a slightly wiser, if more cynical, priest.

Soon afterwards, there was another appeal from the pulpit asking families in the parish to consider taking boys on parole into their homes at weekends. A special type of family was needed here: perhaps an elderly couple, the husband a retired schoolmaster or foreman, the wife rich in the teenage experience of her own children, neither of them gullible, but large-hearted and sensible. At four o'clock the same afternoon, there was a ring at the presbytery. "I asked my mother," said a girl of fourteen from a lapsed family, "and she said, 'Yes, any time,' so would you put our name down." There were no other rings.

Were you to visit this "plum of a parish" today, you would probably fail to see any signs of disintegration. Masses still start on time; slightly stern, but polite, gentlemen still show you to your seat; the mothers still meet regularly over a cup of tea on Wednesday afternoons and arrange the next pilgrimage, the decorators in their white coats are giving the rectory its customary cleaning. The parish will no doubt remain standing for another hundred years, provided, of course, there are no more bombs.

We all know the average parishioners in parish life: they very seldom give their clergy any trouble. They come to Sunday Mass regularly, frequently receive the sacraments, like to have their homes consecrated to the Sacred Heart, insist on Catholic schools for their children, have great respect and loyalty for their clergy, are a bit careless about Sunday newspapers, never budge on their stand against divorce, don't like becoming involved in arguments about the Faith.

The average parishioner has so long been called the salt of the earth by the clergy that, with the constant repetition, the phrase has lost some of its meaning. "I've got the best lot of parishioners you could ask for," one parish priest will say. One might retort: "What have you got them for?" A parish may be a "plum," but plums live a much different kind of existence from salt. What exactly, one may ask, is the function of such a "plum of a parish"? Is it there merely to carry out an organizational or administrative role in the diocese? Or has it a mission of some kind? Are those Masses celebrated every Sunday morning just to make sure that people have the opportunity of hearing Mass, or does this repetitive sacrificial meal have an animating effect in the local community?

These parishioners give the parish clergy no trouble. They don't make scenes during the sermon; they don't tip up the basket when it comes round to them; they don't disagree when the bishop sends them a new parish priest. Certainly all this is admirable. But shouldn't the clergy be troubled more—about such things as the lack of response to such an emergency as the arrival of the Hungarian boys? What of the large number of neglected or illegitimate children in Catholic homes? Should not some disquiet be felt when Catholic Christians absolve themselves from any further responsibility by putting a silver coin in the collection basket?

There is the true story of a German bishop who was making a visitation of a parish in his diocese. He arrived to find the village gaily decorated and festooned in his honor. All the parishioners were lining the streets to receive him. At the banquet given in his honor, he stood up. "On my way here," he said, "I stopped my car to speak to a beggar who had just left your village. He told me that he had been to every house here asking for food. You were so intent on receiving me as your bishop that no one had time to spare for the beggar, and he left you empty-handed. Here before me is a sumptuous banquet, in my honor. I thank you for all your love and devotion to me, but I am bitterly disappointed in you. I came in all my robes and glory as the representative of Christ. The beggar came in all his rags and destitution and you received him not." And with these words the bishop left them.

Many English Catholic parishioners have been asked why they are so hesitant in receiving African students into their homes, reluctant to adopt fatherless babies. Always they say that the risk is too grave. A better answer would be that their Christian formation has been too superficial. When demands, outside of normal parish procedure, are made upon their faith and charity, they display a spiritual destitution. When they are faced with problems demanding a personal solution rather than the impersonal mechanical one of an organized body, a lack of depth in their own personal qualities is apparent.

All this implies that high on the list of parish priorities today is the need to form, from an amorphous mass of parishioners, specialized groups ready to give unstintingly to whatever human need confronts them. Often, in recent years particularly, one notices that many human contemporary problems are side-stepped and given a merely superficial solution, for the curious reason that Christian life in the parish has become overorganized.

Today the average parish does not lack organization. Its techniques have sufficiently evolved over the last hundred years to meet the need of any organized show of strength. Wembley Stadium and the Royal Albert Hall will never remain empty when it is a matter of a Catholic rally or protest meeting; football pools and bingos will for some time to come increase rather than decrease their profits; sociological surveys and door-to-door censuses will never lack zealots to man them.

The danger is that in concern for the organized life of the Church, the organic life of a parish may be gradually stifled out of existence. Cardinal Suhard of Paris used to complain that in his diocese he had too many administrators—and not enough priests. But his sigh need not necessarily be used only as a stick to beat the clergy. One could as easily use it to condemn the laity for hiding the light of *their* priesthood behind the superstructure of their organized membership of the Church. As the moral and spiritual needs of mankind increase in our highly involved way of life, so, too, does the parish need to adapt its life to meet these needs. It will supply them, not in terms of numbers, but in those of individual persons in the community who will revitalize local social life with the strength of their Christian conviction and the degree of their pastoral competence.

Missionary parishes are not those always running schemes to add to the numerical or ideological strength of the

Church, but those which mirror the life and love of the Triune God. These are missionary in that they continue and complete through the parish community the complementary missions of the Son of God and of the Holy Spirit. The divine missions were to bring men fullness of life.

A bishop erects a parish in any given area for the same divine purpose. When the life it brings cannot be recognized for the techniques employed to convey that life in abundance, then it is time to sacrifice an inordinate love of structure for the sake of inner development and growth, solidity for the sake of spontaneity, stability for the sake of fertility. A "plum of a parish" might discover that in becoming missionary it had considerably enhanced its prestige. The worrying stirrings among its foundations might easily turn into a stirring of new life.

2

Requiem for a Parish

<hr>

*The supernatural is all the more
capable of perfecting nature the
less it aims at taking its place.*
GUSTAVE THIBON

Has the parish had its day?

When a preliminary Gallup poll was undertaken to gauge
reactions to the question, die-hards among the clergy and
laity refused even to admit the possibility of the question,
while the devil-may-care type used it to throw a few stones
at existing practice and procedure. If there was to be a
genuine question and hope for an authentic answer, factual
evidence had to be provided, offering a true interpretation
of the parish in contemporary society.

A measure of historical research was needed. It turned
out to be no great task, because the parish as we know it
today is of very short duration and its records, though
scanty, are easily available. All it meant was turning over
the files of parish bulletins and registers for the last fifty
years or so, examining the questions asked in official dioce-

san forms over the same period, collecting the impressions of clergy of three generations to assess any changes in seminary training, and discovering the social changes which have come about recently in the contemporary scene.

The method of inquiry had to be historical. Only against the background of its own history and that of the society in which it existed could one judge whether or not the parish of today was carrying out a Christian mission *in its own proper context* or in the actuality of its own situation.

The historical method employed has, of course, been used with great success in the biblical and liturgical fields. With the Bible particularly, it has come to be taken for granted that a right understanding of a particular event or text depends almost always on the context in which it happened or was given. So, too, in an estimate of the position of the parish in contemporary society, it is a matter of some importance to discover whether the method of its mission is appropriate to the contemporary context. By examining its history over a period of fifty to a hundred years, one is in a position to judge whether the method is contemporary or has been carried into the present from the past.

The relevance, therefore, of the question: *Has the parish had its day?* may now be more apparent. We must consider the possibility that accepted parish procedure and practice may be adapted to a situation which no longer exists. Such a parish may have had its day because it has still to come to terms with the present day and is disregarding certain creative possibilities open to it, through a too slavish attachment to the conventions of the past.

Perhaps we seem to be placing too much reliance on the evidence from parish records, which in themselves concern the administrative more than the human life of a parish. So much more happens in the life of a parish, it may be objected, than what is recorded in parish bulletins or announced from parish pulpits. This is undoubtedly true, but is it not also true that the attitudes adopted by the average parishioner toward his parish affiliation and the obligations imposed on him as a member of a parish are determined in the main by the kind of inspiration (or lack of inspiration) he finds expressed through church notices, parish bulletins and diocesan forms?

· *The Evidence* ·

1. From the files of parish bulletins and registers the following information was collected. Parish visiting is still conducted in the same manner, and indeed with the same sense of urgency, as it has been for over fifty years. In certain parishes, a list of the streets to be visited in the coming week was a prominent item in the weekly notices appearing regularly week after week and year after year. In more than one bulletin the phrase "the eighth sacrament of the door-knocker" suggested that this parish activity had rated very high in parish priorities, consistently, ever since the parish had been founded. Regarding parish confraternities, the evidence showed that fashions changed regularly. The Holy Family Confraternity, for instance, which enjoyed

great popularity well into the twentieth century had, by the 1920's, almost completely disappeared. The Christian Doctrine Confraternity could be identified under many different guises, though seldom mentioned as such. That of the Blessed Sacrament had field days most years, but was most successful in the 1930's. The Children of Mary have met over the whole period under investigation, but with gradually depleted numbers. The Union of Catholic Mothers and the Catholic Women's League have benefited from the rise in the standard of living and to some extent have taken over from the parish Mothers' Meeting. Whether they add more vitality to the parish is an open question, though they do seem to have broken through some of the class barriers existing in some parishes. Parish socials and concerts, men's clubs, annual outings no longer play so large a part in parish life, though parish pilgrimages are becoming increasingly popular. The St. Vincent de Paul Conference is still an honored grouping and seems not to have suffered from an active Legion of Mary. Bingo and football pools, likewise, have not dispensed with the Christmas bazaar and summer garden fete. Evening Masses help to ease the congestion of the late Sunday morning Mass. Sermons have become much shorter and are now termed instructions. In the main, the parish societies and organizations which were in existence at the turn of the century still continue to supply the needs of young and old.

The overall picture is rather a dull one, its details sparse and uninspiring. The notices for the week beginning March 4, 1923, are very much like those for April 5, 1959; the bulletins for June, 1912, could have been reproduced in

July, 1957, with very few changes. The impression given from this source of evidence was that the happenings and events in the life of an average parish conform to a blueprint which left the drawing board toward the end of the pontificate of Pope Leo XIII. Apart from minor adjustments, the established pattern of today's parochial life answers the needs of a nineteenth-century community; it still has to adapt itself to the mind of St. Pius X and the new pastoral needs he uncovered, and even more so to the greater changes in Catholic outlook inspired by Pius XI. Implementation of the suggestions, indeed instructions of Pius XII and the imagination of John XXIII remain in the future.

2. Though a parish may often appear to be a self-contained community, the pattern and scope of its life and action is determined in certain respects by the diocese which is, in fact, the normal unit of government in the Church, parish priests being assistants of the bishop and parishes offshoots of the diocesan see or seat of government. Evidence, therefore, was sought from the fact-finding forms which diocesan authorities circulate at various times to keep themselves informed about the situation, e.g., at a time of visitation, before granting faculties and dispensations, during a crisis in denominational education.

Very little change has been made in the last half century in the format of these questionnaires. The information they require is mainly statistical or in the interests of the canon law of the Church. Individual Catholic life is seen in terms of a legalistic or canonical one; success of the Catholic mission is measured numerically.

The form to be filled in making an application to receive a catechumen into the Church is especially revealing. The word used is "reconciliation," implying that the average catechumen has at some time in his life quarreled with the Church. The main condition laid down for the reconciliation is that the catechumen solemnly promises to accept the teaching and legislative authority of the Church, suggesting that those outside the Church up to now have remained outside for so long because they have believed this authority in faith and morals to have rested in some other Christian body or in the House of Parliament. Undoubtedly this was the situation when such an application form was first issued, but it is not the situation in England today. It is interesting to note here that recently in France it was decided to remove the words "re-christianization" and de-christianization from the Catholic vocabulary and to speak in future only of "christianization." In England, a similar realistic move could be made by refraining from referring to *Catholic* and *non-Catholic*, as though everyone could be conveniently pigeonholed into these two exclusive categories, since the majority of people have no Christian denominational affiliation.

The strongly emphasized concern shown for the teaching claims of the Church seems slightly unrealistic, since no complementary hint is given that a future member of the Church has to play a much fuller role in her life than a mere passive observance; the *human* contribution which a prospective member of the Church has to make to her organic life is neither commented upon nor requested.

3.   The third source of information came from the dioce-

san seminary by way of the clergy who had been trained there in the last fifty years. Until fairly recently—that is, for clergy in their forties and upwards—spiritual formation and the presentation of Catholic doctrine appears to have followed a norm in existence for the three centuries since the Council of Trent. The enemies of the Church were mainly Luther, Calvin, and Zwingli; the main issue was *ex opere operato*. Only lately has the thesis "De Ecclesia" ceased to be a minor thesis in an apologetics course and become the pivotal doctrine of the whole theological system. The "craze" (as it has been described) for the Mystical Body has also led to some withdrawal from an erstwhile emphasis on individual sacerdotal sanctity and stress placed on a genuine missionary spirituality.

As yet, however, there are few signs that the clergy being educated in our seminaries know how to integrate the laity into the total mission of the Church, how to give them a proper lay holiness, or, indeed, how to effect in concrete the theory of the "complementariness" of clergy and laity in spirituality and action. There seems to be an unfortunate tendency to confuse method with technique: one of the recent innovations is to bring diocesan canonists into the seminary in the last year of the course to explain the filling out of forms and suchlike. There is no contact with committed and competent laity already engaged in working out a new method in communicating the supernatural message of Christianity to a secularized society. Most young priests leaving the seminaries today believe they have all the right answers; nobody as yet is coming into the seminaries to acquaint them with a different set of questions or to tell

them that their right answers are but the right answers to
the wrong questions.

4. This is why a fourth source of information appears
vitally necessary—the *actual* situation in which the Church
is placed and which she seeks to animate. What changes,
if any, have come about in the social scene in the last century during which the average parish has been in existence?
Have these changes affected the problems or obstacles facing both the Church and the people whom she seeks to
serve? Is the nature of these problems such that they offer
the parish enhanced opportunities for being *present* in the
life of the times?

The main change which has come about in our exploding
society is in the *human condition* itself. There has been a
gradual diminution of the human person *qua* person, a
situation due fundamentally to the fact that, of the elements
which go to make up a healthy human condition, that of
labor, has been detached from the natural hierarchy and
made the dominant inspiration of modern industrialized
and urbanized life. Modern man has in fact been dispos-
sessed of his proper *earthly* condition, become alienated
from the world in which he has been providentially constituted, and is without roots. He lacks that minimum of human altitude from which to take off into the supernatural.
Pope Pius XII, when drawing mankind's attention to the
overriding superstition, observed that the artificially created
hierarchy of scientific production was turning the human
person into a mere means to a technological end: he was
being attacked at the very center of human dignity and
freedom. All this has an important bearing on the nature

and meaning of the Church's contemporary mission. How far, we must ask, does the mission of the average parish today concern itself with Pius XII's description of the essence of this mission, i.e., the growth of the human person living in society to his full maturity and development? Is it completely tracking down the deep root causes of spiritual *acedia*, aware of the emotional starvation its people are experiencing in the new world of total work, conscious of the need of collaborating with those other elements in the social organism which form the human person? Is it intent on finding a new synthesis of the natural and supernatural orders through which the individual person, the family and the community of the twentieth century will discover new forms to measure up to the new challenges to their existence and function?

· A Case of Arrested Development ·

The second stage in an historical inquiry such as this is to seek in history the reasons why, in view of the above evidence, there appears to be some arrestment in the organic growth and development of an average parish. The fact that one speaks today of growth and development in the parish, not in terms of bricks and mortar, but of a living organism, means that the way we have to judge the meaning and function of a parish is very different from the way to which we have been accustomed. We have been forced to raise our sights and to re-examine the credentials of the parish.

"Human reality," writes Julian Marias, "differs radically from the biological organism because the latter, once constituted, functions in a stable and 'permanent' way, so that modifications of itself emerge from its previous structure or *nature*, while what is human only fulfills itself in the form of a happening of time." [1]

After penal times in England, it is understandable why security and acceptance became dominant moods in Catholic life. Such moods do not necessarily conflict with a concern for souls but can open the way for ossification. If one can detect, in the strongly organized and efficiently administered parish of today, a certain lack of resilience and flexibility, one must first judge it in comparison with times far different from ours. The Church in nineteenth-century England had to work with all-but-nonexistent resources in trained men, in means of training, and in money (as Monsignor Philip Hughes puts it). Its struggle to secure the material basis of life was a full-time anxiety. To perpetuate the mood of nineteenth-century Catholicism in our own times, however, would savor somewhat of ancestor worship. We would also be employing our far greater resources, both of trained men and of means of training, for ends no more enlightened than those of our safety-first forefathers.

In passing judgment on diocesan procedure in the matter of fact-finding forms, one cannot find fault with the care and attention given to implementing the requirements of those sessions of the Council of Trent which established

[1] Julian Marias, *Reason and Life* (New Haven: Yale University Press, 1956).

the juridical or legal status of the parish. But, again, these sessions (Sessions XXI and XXIV in particular) need to be interpreted in their historical context. Their purpose was to restore order in the confusion surrounding such matters as the appointment of parish priests, parish boundaries, and parish benefices; this confusion was a legacy from feudal times, and in the new age of the Renaissance church government needed a clearer definition. The new canon law was never, however, viewed as an end in itself, but for the spiritual interests of the people.

So, too, with the ecclesiology of the Council of Trent which was predominantly anti-Lutheran and in defense of hierarchic government and authority. The need of the time was to defend the whole meaning of the hierarchical apostolate of the Church against those who denied one of its essential elements and would confine it entirely to the care of the laity. It seems today almost a *volte-face* when modern Popes continually demand the participation of the laity in the Church's hierarchical apostolate, speak of the laity as in the front ranks of her contemporary mission, and maintain that without the laity she cannot today become the vital unifying principle in contemporary society.

To think and act as if the crisis facing the Church today is identical with that of the sixteenth century would be to deny all development in human history, to fossilize the Church in a medieval setting. Today we can see that, as a more highly developed and enriched ecclesiology replaces the former anti-Lutheran version, future parish procedure and practice will be recast on the anvil of the laity. A "kept" laity can no longer be the norm of parish life. The more mature the laity becomes, the more a parish becomes truly present in its local society. If at the moment there is still confusion about the respective rights of clergy and laity in the mission of the parish, most of the blame for this lies in the fact that we still think of the Church in terms of her structure and ideology and have lost a sense of her organic mission. An authentic lay apostolate can never be confined to mere parish administration, or restrict the co-partnership of the layman to being merely "the hands and feet" of the clergy. Only by establishing the rights of the laity in the temporal order will the "complementariness" of the clergy and laity be seen in terms, not of rivalry, but of collaboration.

The tendency of recent English Catholic life to carry the past into the present, and to work at a tangent from the main stream of ecclesial adaptation to contemporary life, is most easily seen at the moment of the changeover from the artisan to the scientific mode of work; 1851 is recognized as a crucial date in England's development into the first of the new Industry States. Psychologically the English Catholic body was unprepared for such a change. The Vicars Apostolic who had guided the fortunes of the Church before the restoration of the English hierarchy in 1850 were in the tradition of the Catholic landed gentry. Though Catholic life became more and more centered in the towns and cities of the "New England" during the nineteenth century, Catholic mentality did not adapt itself sufficiently to the revolution taking place in English social life and was surprisingly unperceptive of the deeply underlying problems present in the changes. For many years the wind from the Industry State was for the Catholic body in the east. It was the Nonconformists, with their strong lay tradition, who did most to humanize and christianize the rapidly evolving new world of total work: and in the last analysis it can now be seen that it was Cardinal Newman who was better informed about the nature of the Catholic Christian mission to contemporary society than Cardinal Manning, despite the latter's involvement in the fray. For the most part, the English Catholic body remained as refugees within the existing situation. Only in recent times, when the contemporary scientific mode of work is determining the syllabuses of England's Catholic schools, have Catholic educational authorities become concerned about the lack of personal formation in a national system of education geared to supplying industrialism with a sufficiency of manually dexterous and mentally agile workers. Yet for over seventy years the majority of Catholic children in elementary schools have had little or no *specific* Christian preparation for their entry into the world of contemporary work. They have suffered continually from the lack of a faith which would offer them some interpretation of this adult world.

We are accustomed to judge the success of the English Catholic mission to the nineteenth century in terms of organization and building development: 439 churches and nearly 1,400 schools were built in the period 1851-1874. But as Monsignor Philip Hughes remarks: "For priests, as for people, the schools could not be a whole-time anxiety that left little leisure for the study of the ultimate causes of the ills of time, a preoccupation which badly hindered the growth of the desiderated contemplative attitude."[1] We might ask today: can such preoccupation continue to conceal from English Catholics the need for establishing a new harmony of the three basic elements in the social organism: work, art, and religion? Each of these elements has an organic function to play in the making of a healthy social organism and each element carries out this rôle by way of collaboration with the others. Work, art, and religion do not exist for their own sakes, but for the sake of the human person who is the origin and end of all social life.

Only an arrested development in her organic life can account for the historical fact that at the moment of the great changeover in our society—from the artisan to the scientific mode of work—the Church failed to adapt her divine principle of life to the changing human situation and to devise new forms of collaboration between the Christian religion and the contemporary mode of work. It is not surprising, therefore, if today we can recognize in her policy, practice, and procedure, certain of the misconceptions about the meaning of human existence on this earth present in modern industrialized society, for where the work of adaptation is left undone, members of the Church are an easy prey to the faulty ideals of a society which has come to birth without her. A phenomenon, which we can afford to forget only at our peril, is that the form of society we know today is one that has come into existence without Christian inspiration; its whole impetus has come from the

[1] Msgr. Philip Hughes, *English Catholics* (London: Burns and Oates).

new modern belief that the stability and security of all social life depend absolutely on an ever-mounting spiral of social production and that, in this "vocation of our times," professional qualifications deputize for personal qualities.

Josef Pieper indicates the proportions of the changes which have come about in the social scene:

An erroneous or defective interpretation of the reality of existence inevitably gives rise to faulty goals and faulty ideals. For, as all things must be grounded in being, so must the guideposts of action be rooted in the knowledge of reality. True to this general law, enlightened liberalism (this widespread and intricate, yet fundamentally uniform network of misinterpretations of the objective reality of man which has stamped with its distinctive mark the century now fading into the irretrievable past) inevitably produced a disastrous distortion of the ideas of ethical man. This distortion falsifies and deprives of their reality the very concepts in which Western Christianity has come to summarize the due and proper image of man: prudence, justice, fortitude, and temperance.[1]

It will suffice, we think, to draw attention to one deficiency in average parish procedure and practice to show how far contemporary Christian life and action have been infected with modern secularized values. This is the absence of the natural virtue of prudence. The natural hierarchy of the cardinal virtues has been forgotten to such an extent that it has become customary to give the highest ranking to the two lowest virtues: fortitude and temperance. Yet

[1] Josef Pieper, *Fortitude and Temperance* (New York: Pantheon, 1954).

prudence is the mold and mother of all the other cardinal virtues, and "none but the prudent man can be just, brave, and temperate, and the good man is good in so far as he is prudent." [1]

Avoiding the modern danger of confusing prudence with timorous small-minded self-preservation, or a selfish concern about oneself (both unworthy of the noble man), and defining it as the direction of volition and action toward truth, one can see that all the efforts and sacrifices made within a parish to serve the Christian community avail very little unless these are directed toward each member of the community reaching his true goal as a member of the Church and finding his own truth as someone of unique and irreplaceable value in God's plans of creation and redemption.

To think of the parish as less than an organism, to be content with a kind of spiritual proletariat in the parish, to deny the people the means of bringing to their parish community a love no less than a love of the *whole* Church (e.g., through soft-pedaling the "foreign" missions as though these were sucking away the resources of the parish), to fail to recognize the modern lay apostolate as an indispensable means of raising their status in the Church from that of a mere "practicing" to a "witnessing" member of the Church, to abstain from examining the situation in which the parish exists in order to make it more organically present in its local society: all these suggest that vast imprudences are occurring in the name of the Christian religion.

[1] Josef Pieper, *Prudence* (New York: Pantheon, 1959).

• *Continuity and Development* •

Prudence demands that in these times, when the rallying call should be "no continuity without development," there should be a reconsidering of the *proper* mission of the parish in contemporary society. In order that one may find the answer to this question, research needs to be carried out in both the social and the theological fields. Correct information is required concerning the situation in which the mission of the parish has to be conducted; we have to be sure, also, what we mean by the *missionary* rôle of a parish in the modern Church.

Valuable light is thrown on the problem by examining the history of the Church at the moment when this crisis of growth which we have been discussing first made itself felt; during those very critical years for the Church, Bishop Challoner was in command. Wishing to perpetuate the memory of the seminary and religious priests of penal times, Challoner wrote his *Memoirs of Missionary Priests.* He did so in order that what they had accomplished should become part of a living tradition and, as such, throw much-needed light on, and indeed indicate, the direction that English Catholicism should follow.

Challoner is an historically significant figure because he arrived on the scene at a time when great changes were taking place in the structure of the English Catholic body, and he identified these changes for what they really were, as heralding a crisis of growth for the Church. With the

Catholic Relief Act and its promise of full emancipation, the Catholic landed gentry, who had proven the main bulwark of Catholic life during the years of persecution, began to drop their heavy load of responsibility. The "Roman oases," those pockets of Catholic community life which were the secret of survival, began in Challoner's time to break up. The "new people" of the cities and towns, and from Ireland, were to take over from the landed gentry.

Since these "Roman oases" were the equivalent of the parish of today, it is valuable to see to what degree co-partnership then existed between clergy and laity. The laity in penal times became responsible for keeping open the lines of communication, for supplying vital information about the situation, for making the necessary contacts between the missionary priests and those in need of their ministrations. Priests arriving in this country from abroad could not, without such lay help, hope to carry out a successful mission, let alone survive for any length of time.

In the circumstances, however, it was inevitable that the laity (and the only responsible laity were those of the landed class) became the dominant half of the partnership. The mission of the Church in these times was the limited one of survival and preservation. (The measure of its success in this mission can be seen by comparing the situation in this country today with that of the Scandinavian countries, where during penal times following the Reformation there was no such partnership and no stream of priests entering from seminaries and religious houses abroad.) Within its own limitations, the partnership between laity and clergy which evolved during penal times was most successful.

Yet what was effective within the limits of a persecuted Church could not hope to survive *in the same form* in the changed conditions of the nineteenth century. With the end of the penal laws came greater freedom of movement, a greater independence of action for the clergy, a lessening of tension for the laity. With all this came new problems, new opportunities, new challenges. In theory, of course, the degree of partnership which had come to exist between clergy and laity should have adapted itself to these new conditions, become deeper and more enriched. In fact, it tended to dissolve, for a variety of reasons, not the least being that the "new people" of the cities and towns identified by Challoner as taking over the mantle from the landed gentry had yet to be educated for completely new responsibilities.

This crisis of growth for the Church which appeared at the close of the eighteenth century has still to be resolved. That it can be so resolved only according to the same living tradition, the Church's tradition, of the missionary priests and the laity of penal times in England cannot be denied. But to be resuscitated, this tradition must be constantly adapted to the new and far different conditions of our own times. Today the people of the Church are more *present* in the life of society than at any other time in her history.

In many ways, the mission which a modern industrialized city parish carries out today, is far more perplexing than that of penal times. To understand and to be understood by the society which it seeks to animate is a task which the modern parish finds increasingly more difficult. All the more important, therefore, that, in the face of such complexity, it avoids the dangers of the easy answer or of oversimplification.

For many years the Catholic question in England has been seen in terms of continuity. Against the claims of rival Churches and Christian ideologies, the Catholic Church has laid most stress on her identity as the one, true Church of Christ. Against all comers, she has admitted no compromise in her claims to be the divine institution set up on earth by Christ and endowed with His own divine authority.

Continuity, however, also implies development. Indeed, in our times, continuity means very little unless it is proposed in terms of a living organism. To continue today with all her claims intact, the Church must grow. The past insistence on her structure needs now to be better balanced with an equal concern for her organic development.

In view of the great changes which have come about in the structure of modern society and in the thinking habits of its members, it would be misrepresenting the Church to present her, either in her total mission or in her parish mission, as tied irrevocably to unchanging methods or routines. It would misrepresent her because it would be interpreting her divine principles of life in merely human terms. The Church is unchanging, but not in her human manifestation. The transcendence of her inner divine essence demands that she continually adapt herself to the exigencies of time and place. In this sense, therefore, she is always changing. Such changes in her visible structure and in her methods are signs of life and fertility. Where they do not appear there is evidence of stultification and decline.

A short time ago, a number of parochial clergy met to discuss parish priorities. These priests were worried, not by the difficulty of manning the Sunday Masses, but by the measures they should take to extend their own availability to the people. They saw a shortage of clergy, not in terms of a mathematical insufficiency, but in those of a pastoral inadequacy. They had come, not to discuss how one priest could do the work of two, but how each of them could carry out a more effective and competent apostolate.

The discussion was jeopardized from the start by the assumption that the main issue was one of recasting parish priorities in order to make better use of existing time. There was no initial questioning of the nature of the mission of a parish, of the nature of the service it gives to the community, or how this service can never remain static, but must correspond to ever-changing needs and ever-growing opportunities of the people. Only when this point had been clarified could any rearrangement in the multifarious activities of a parish be attempted. Not the *bonum utile* but the *bonum honestum* was the main issue.

The parish mirrors the Church. The extent of its action is determined for it by the nature and scope of the action of the contemporary Church. One or two definitions from Pope Pius XII lend much needed exactitude and decisiveness to the rôle of the parish today.

To define the Church merely in terms of her organization and ideology is to misrepresent her: she is more than an organization or ideology, she is an organism.[1]

The Church knows that her mission, though by its proper nature and aims belonging to the religious and moral spheres and taking its place in the life beyond and in eternity, nevertheless reaches into the very heart of human history. Always and everywhere, by unceasingly adapting herself to circumstances of time and place, she seeks to mold in accordance with the law of Christ, the individual person so that by doing so she builds the moral foundations of life in society.

Today, then, we cannot be content with a definition of *catholic* or *missionary* confined to a quantitative or geographical extension of the Church. We have to see the Church as missionary in an organic sense. This has a greater affinity to the more precise meaning of the word *universal* as a gathering-together-in-oneness (uni-versal). The Church does not so much spread outward as draw inward. She is more a "presence" in the world than a widespread organization. The more she is present in the life of the world as its underlying principle of unity, the more evident is the fact that her action is supremely that of animation. She does not usurp, dominate, impose, or destroy; she fulfils. She supplies contemporary social life with the only sufficiently spiritual inspiration or impetus, and this will bring it to its final term as the way of life in which the people who enjoy it will find their highest aspirations as human beings.

[1] Pius XII, Address to the Tenth World Congress of Historical Sciences, English trans. *Catholic Documents*, Vol. 20 (Pontifical Court Club, 1956).

• *The True Meaning of a Missionary Parish* •

That is why today, in defining Catholic as missionary, we can speak of every parish in the Church as a missionary parish since it has come into existence to partake in the total mission of the Church; and this is to form man in his wholeness. We can speak, therefore, of the mission of every parish as a total mission in two senses: firstly, because it shares the whole apostolate of the Church, secondly, because it is concerned with the whole of human life.

It shares the whole apostolate of the Church. The nature and scope of its activity are determined for it by those of the Church. Its interests, ambitions, and ideals are wide-embracing as those of the Church. If it did not have these aims and ambitions, it would compromise its action within its own territory; it would cease to act with the action of the Church; it would come to exist on the fringe of authentic Catholic life.

It is concerned with the whole of human life. It embraces the human person in the whole of his life, his personal and religious life, his social, public, and political life, his cosmic and material life.

The term *Catholic*, used to denote a parish in the Church, has more than a juridical or legal sense. A parish in the Church is Catholic, not merely or primarily because it has been officially erected in a certain locality, but because the action it carries out in that locality is that of the Church. A Catholic parish carries out an organic role in society. It works within an already existing society in order to animate it. Its action is primarily one of collaboration. It does not take the place of the society in which it carries out its work of animation or take its subjects out of that society, but gradually transforms that society through the fertilizing action of its divine principle of life and by making its subjects more *present* as members of that society. To do this, it works with all those other elements in the social organism to form a way of life in which the human person will best attain his highest aspirations; it finds with them a method of collaboration through which each part of the unity will combine in spirit and technique, not for its own isolated glorification, but for the growth and maturation of the person.

This sacramental and mystical existence of the Church may be distinguished from her juridical and legal existence. This aspect of the Church's life can never be more than secondary to her organic existence. It exists to serve the interests of her organic mission. All the Church's machinery of government presupposes a deeper apostolate which is to bring the human person in the community to full maturity.

Nonetheless, these two forms of existence of the Church complement each other. The organizational apostolate makes effective the organic rôle of the Church in society: her organic rôle gives meaning and form to her organizational life. The divine life which the Church brings to humanity needs all the organizational aids available to her, but these are not ends in themselves; rather, in a constantly changing and highly variegated human condition, they need to be adapted and related constantly to the mode of her organic presence in society. The Church may take years to perfect her organization, only to find eventually that the human situation for which she has organized has changed radically and that she must find new methods, techniques, and organizational aids.

Sometimes it is difficult to recognize the organic missionary action of the Church behind the involved machinery of Church government and the intricate system of Christian doctrine. When this is the case, the reverse side of the coin is a Christian people deprived of a Christian eschatology, no longer on the move, filling in time, instead of filling time with God. Deprived of a genuine hope, their Christian life is a permanent evasion of reality. Conforming rather than behaving, they can supply their society with no true interpretation of the times in which they live.

It may well be asked why today we have begun to think again of the Church in terms of her organic life rather than in those of her organization and ideology. The explanation is to be found in the Chuch's situation today. Her growth and development as a divine-human reality do not take place independently of her situation in the world. On the contrary, the rate of this growth is in proportion to the depth of the changes taking place in the human condition and to her ability to understand the nature of these changes. "To understand and to be understood" is the first principle of her missionary action.

Greater changes have taken place in the human condition in the last hundred years than in the whole of the preceding three thousand. History, Canon Dondeyne explains, is not simply a butterfly pattern of whimsical happenings without sequence and order, but basically the history of the progressive emancipation of man and mankind. The three conditions for this progressive liberation are: the progress of positive science and industrial technique (labor and work in the human organism), a more genuine recognition of man by man (*vita activa*), and the education of man (*vita contemplativa*). No one can deny that today the possibilities open to man have been enormously increased and his horizons considerably widened. For the first time in human history, as an example, the idea has arisen that access to the benefits of civilization and culture is possible for great numbers of people; a mass liberation of the human person is no longer considered a Utopian vision.

Only by considering the Church as an historical reality can we recognize that what is happening in the world today has considerably enlarged and deepened her mission. She cannot sit back and watch a new world-humanism come to birth without her inspiration. On the contrary, as mother of all true humanism and civilization, she must go along with and within it. She wants the best for the children of God, not only in the world to come, but on this earth. If she is to continue to preach a genuine Christianity, then it must be one whereby the Christian becomes the most engaged and the most present of men in the span of human history.

That is why Pope Pius XII defined the nature of Christian action today as that of animation. To animate means to recognize the creative possibilities in any given human situation, and to bring men living in that situation to such a degree of human maturity that they become capable of recognizing and responding to these possibilities and through their reply actualizing them to enrich and perfect human life in society.

Today the Church is not merely concerned with defending her structure and ideology against rival Christian organizations and ideologies. She is living largely in post-Christian times, in a world which is coming into existence without Christ (and, as Cardinal Suhard wrote, "The greatest mistake the Christians of the twentieth century could make would be to let this world come to birth and be unified without them"). The great range of scientific discovery and of technical advancement, the tremendous increase in the techniques of human communication through press, cinema, radio, and television, the coming together of the nations of the world in a new internationalism: all these are having enormous effects on the way ordinary people view and value their lives. The mission of the Church is now much larger than securing sectarian advantage or ecclesiastical privilege. It concerns the very fabric of human existence. Her task is to preserve the identity of the human person as an end in himself, not only to preserve, but also to bring to birth an age of a *new* person, one who will be able to find in himself the resources to maintain his God-given dignity and freedom in face of the challenges he finds in the modern technological age.

A fact seldom adverted to by Christians who are expected to be the animators of their society today is the peculiar and strange *other-worldliness* of our modern highly industrialized way of life. Some identify it as the revenge of the forgotten truth of a Christian sacramental view of the world. So rationalized has Christianity become that in despair modern man has transferred his allegiance to a bogus other-worldliness symbolized in Hiroshima and the landing of a man-made *sputnik* on the mountains of the moon. Industrialism has deprived modern man of playing an organic rôle in the making of his society. Now he has become an anonymous nobody and a mere cog in the machine of production. He can no longer believe in himself as a person with a personal contribution to make to the enrichment of the world through the human value of his work and the intelligibility of his human relationships. Deprived of the source of his mysterious existence as a co-worker with God, he has lost sight of the objective reality of life on this earth and seeks to run away from the fear of his isolation and alienation in an orgy of violence, sensationalism, and eroticism. Fundamentally he is emotionally starved, and like his counterpart in the specific religious sphere where fear of life can often hide behind a mask of piety and devotionalism, modern man will hide his behind the windshield of a supercharged automobile or cycle, on an airplane faster than sound, in the making and testing of hydrogen bombs which can destroy continents and human reproductive faculties, and in listening-in to life among the planets.

The Church cannot assume, as in days past, that her supernatural life of grace can be automatically built into an already existing healthy human condition where the natural hierarchies of work, art, and religion, and of labor, work, the active and the contemplative life, still work. She will find that modern industrialized and urbanized life has dried up man's natural soul, muted the call from deep to deep which is the essence of her Christian mission, and placed obstacles in the way of a full human development which are discernible only to the psychologist and the man of faith.

The contemporary mission of the Church, we are told is, in essence, to form man in his wholeness. The challenge which the Church faces and must accept is one which makes the highest demands on her mystery. If today we see her revealing powers and riches hitherto hidden from the world, and expressing her personality at a greater depth, then we can see it as her answer to a situation with which she has never previously been confronted.

• *A Creative Treatment of Reality* •

As a unit of the Church, the parish in contemporary society has also "to understand and to be understood." To carry out an authentic existence in the Church it, too, must think and love with the mind and heart of the Church. Otherwise, it will hide behind the façade of its juridical or canonical existence and be content to live on the periphery of the Church's mission. How, then, in the midst of present-day complexity and confusion, will the parish organism best serve the interests of the community? It must be by recognition of the fact that any failure of which it is conscious arises not from lack of organizational ability or administrative efficiency, but from an inability to recognize and exploit certain new creative possibilites challenging its existence in the contemporary situation. Some of these bear examination.

PARISH VISITING

Though Archbishop Mathew once wrote that the high
barrier dividing Catholics and non-Catholics has of late
been topped with the "broken glass" of Roman Catholic
moral teaching on the nature and purpose of marriage,
such a barrier does not exist in reality. The day of the
"Roman oases" has passed (and even in those days there
was a good deal of fraternizing between those on either
side of the wall), and the Catholic "ghetto" survives only
in the back-street location of the churches of those times.
Today, Catholics in modern city and suburban parishes do
not form a natural community. In many instances, there is
no community in existence; but where any "natural grouping" is to be found, it is built around work, class, or social
requirements. Since education (in its wider sense of personal formation) is primarily the affair of the community, the
supernatural mission of a parish (if it is to bear fruit today)
cannot ride roughshod over the "natural grouping" in
which Catholics are fully or in part integrated. On the
contrary, it must build into them and use them as under-
pinning.

The accepted practice of visiting members of the parish
as though their faith and Catholic affiliation had no relation
to the "human grouping" of which they form an organic
part, is a relic of the time when the norm of Catholic life
was seen primarily in the light of a Catholic's juridical or
canonical status. Its aim was to stabilize the Roman Catholic
element, to "check up" on its "practice." This may still be

needed, but here again the *bonum utile* should not masquerade as the *bonum honestum.*

By training the spotlight on the problem of lapsation, we miss the more fundamental weakness in contemporary life, which is not the fact that a good number of baptized Catholics give up the "practice" of their faith sometime during their lives, but that, of those who remain "faithful," very few are committed or competent enough to bear effective witness to Christian truth in their everyday lives. Spiritual immaturity is a problem the Catholic body in this country has never really faced, because it is still thinking in terms of juridical, and not of organic, membership of the Church.

It would seem, therefore, that parish visiting would become a far more effective weapon of the parish apostolate if it raised its sights and, far from reinforcing Catholics in their fictitious isolation, concentrated on building up in any given "natural grouping" (a street, a block of flats, a workplace, a coffee-bar) an apostolic Catholic nucleus which, with proper spiritual formation, would become the core of the parish apostolate. Already in some parishes, such groupings exist. Their function is not to proselytize, but as Catholic Christians to become more "present" in the life of their local society, to show the Church as something attractive and compelling and essentially necessary for a full social and human life. Lay apostolic action is so very often presented as something extraordinary, but, authentically, it is a supernatural and creative treatment of actuality, a work of animation, an awakening in the hearts and minds of a local community those creative possibilities which are so seldom recognized or realized. Like the mission of the Church, it is ultimately to bring the individual living in society to his full development and growth according to the mind of the Creator who created and redeemed him, and values him so highly.

Just as in national life, sociologists and others see the only future of our civilization in the gradual raising of the status of our society from an executive to an educational one, so, in the Catholic body, the future mission of Church and parish depends first and foremost on raising the whole status of the individual member of the Church to a level where he becomes responsible for that mission and sees the contribution he makes as interwoven with his own state of life and his own human situation.

HOME AND FAMILY

Industrialism and urbanization remain the key problems awaiting a Christian solution. The effects these had on home and family life are considerable. That is why no parish can be content today with merely accepting as a principle the dictum that the family is the bedrock of civilized living; it has to take steps to ensure that the families which it serves are able to live up to the principle. Extreme care needs to be taken that the contemporary Christian family is able to find within itself the resources needed to face up to the challenges to its unity in modern life.

Here, again, teaching on the family often assumes that we know all there is to know about the form family life has to take in our highly civilized and complicated commercial culture. What worked fifty years or a century ago, we presume, still works today. The aids to family life found in the Catholic Christian affiliation in the last century are imagined to be sufficient for securing and stabilizing family unity today. Yet the very concept of home and family has changed to a remarkable extent, particularly in recent years. Not only has industrialism sent the members of a family into differing trades and professions, but it has also made the safeguarding of the family dependent on a host of institutions and organizations which in varying degrees protect the rights and interests of individual members of the family and of the family itself. We can no longer talk of the home in terms of its own four walls or as an Englishman's castle; home today includes everything which happens to its individual members: trade unions, the national compulsory system of education, the Stock Exchange, the press, cinema, and television.

It is not sufficient to speak of the inviolability of the human family, we must examine the complicated structure of the contemporary family. It is wishful thinking to hanker after a solution to present social and spiritual disintegration without taking into consideration the many social pressures, structures, and institutions which have to be included in the very notion of home and family today.

Nonetheless, the greater the divergence, as Teilhard de Chardin puts it, the higher the degree of convergence. A husband and father who for half his day must engage in all kinds of duplicity and braggadocio to keep his job as a salesman and to win promotion, and for the other half must exercise such contrary qualities as gentleness, understanding, and selflessness in dealing with his wife and children, will find only strain and tension in the situation unless he discovers and fosters in himself a deeper unity, thus harmonizing his Jekyll and Hyde existence.

It is highly significant that very few of such husbands and fathers ever approach their clergy for help in solving such personal problems, and one wonders whether such problems or obstacles to human development are ever seen as such by clergy or laity.

"In conversations about the Faith," writes Josef Goldbrunner, "the primary concern nowadays is not the justification or defense of the Faith, nor is the main emphasis on intellectual understanding. It is Faith as a way of life and a form of life that is sought after, dimly descried, or evaded today." [1]

If the parish in her contemporary mission is to serve the Christian community, it is plainly inadequate that the defense of the home and family be restricted to outbursts from the pulpit or press; considerable time and care have to be given inside the life of the community to assure that the people are helped to rise to the occasion in our highly-involved and richly variegated way of life, and fashion in their own individual and family lives those personal qualities needed today if family unity is to develop.

We have yet to find the norm of family life which measures up to the demands and opportunities in contemporary society. So-called "Catholic" families need to realize that, although their members have been baptized and con-

[1] Josef Goldbrunner, *Cure of Mind and Cure of Soul* (New York: Pantheon, 1958).

secrated to the Sacred Heart, there is no guarantee that they have acquired an automatic guide and inspiration for living a full family life in a society which is constantly depersonalizing its members. There can only be one norm of family life in the parish community today, and that is for the family to rediscover its organic role in the community. That this rôle must be in accordance with the new needs and the new structure of our industrialized and urbanized society needs no emphasis. In short, we need in the parish to form Christian families who are distinguished, not according to the controversies of old, but by the organic and missionary part they play in the evolution of a new community answering contemporary human needs.

SCHOOLS

"The educational revolution of the future," writes Professor Jeffreys, "will be the reintegration of the school into the life of the community." [1] One of the discoveries of the obvious being made today is that the school is but an artificial device in education which is primarily the affair of the community. It is good to remember this in our herculean efforts for the survival of the Catholic school. It will help to give a more exact and decisive direction to our ambitions and planning in this matter.

A question we may well ask today is whether the parish or interparochial school is ever seen in the light of the total contemporary mission of the parish. In short, to what de-

[1] M.V.C. Jeffreys, *Glaucon: An Inquiry into the Aims of Education* (London: Pitman, 1957).

gree is the Catholic school a missionary school in the sense of carrying out an organic role in animating its local society?

Up to now we have been content with seeing the preservation of our schools in terms of self-interest; the great support the Church receives from her people in building Catholic schools is inspired by the principle of the rights of Catholic parents to give their children an education in accordance with their beliefs. In actual fact, this is not the primary reason for having Catholic Christian schools, though very seldom is this mentioned. The rôle a Catholic Christian school plays in the life of the nation is primarily a missionary one, for wherever there is a Catholic school, *there* is a witness to the ideal and necessity of a true Christian upbringing.

Self-interest there must always be, but Christianity advocates *selfless* self-interest. How many of our Catholic people ever see the Catholic school in the light of a missionary witness or beacon in the midst of a completely secularized or indifferent national system of education? If they did, then they could not be satisfied with the merely mediocre, the average ambition: that of being "practicing" Catholics.

We are living in times when the divine in man tends to lose its identity in the avalanche of human effort and achievement. At an exhibition on education and careers organized by the National Union of Teachers, it was noticeable that, whereas God was mentioned, in the kindergarten department, in terms of furry animals and living plants, throughout the rest of the exhibition—with its great bias toward technical and scientific training—He was the great "unmentionable." This was not from any malice, but because we have still to find a way to bring the divine presence and divine providence into contact with modern industrialism and technology. Again, we may ask, how far is the Catholic school forming the young Christians of tomorrow for their future tasks in reopening the lines of communication between eternity and contemporaneity?

When we speak of education for industry, we do not mean supplying operators to work the complex machinery and involved accountancy of the modern age; rather do we mean supplying modern scientific discovery and technical advance with Christians who are sufficiently committed and competent to see that the age of the machine will be accompanied by a new age of the person, who will, as a member of the Church and as her missionary, further the deeper, personal formation of the individual living in society and strengthen him to face the challenge to his freedom, thereby helping him to rise to new heights of personal achievement.

Such a mature Christian can only attain his full growth inside the scene of modern human effort and achievement on the scientific and technical planes. Catholic schooling, therefore, would fail in the present situation, were it to fail in its mission of bringing to birth the embryonic lay apostle and preparing him for his future rôle as animator by giving him a faith which is no less than interpretative of the human scene. The Church forms new types of men and women for the needs of each age. How far, we may ask, are our Catholic schools co-operating in the modern mission of the Church? How can they fully co-operate, unless as parish schools they receive a right direction and a right inspiration from the parish?

PARISH SOCIETIES AND ORGANIZATIONS

"To some extent," writes Bishop Beck, "the existing state of things (among our Catholic societies) hinders the work of Catholic Action." [1] He instances nearly ninety such Catholic societies and organizations, the majority of which came into existence over fifty years ago, all, with scarcely one exception, concerned with a particular aspect of Catholic life or with the interests and activities of a particular Catholic group. What has been said about the Catholic school applies equally well here. It is necessary today to adapt these societies and organizations which bear a Catholic label, to present necessities. No longer is the overriding need of the Church that of self-defense, but to become more present in contemporary society as its underlying and animating principle of unity. All members of Catholic societies need to receive a much more basic training in the modern apostolate; the rules, regulations, traditions, of these societies need to be reviewed in the light of present-day emergencies.

[1] *English Catholics,* edited by Most Rev. G. A. Beck (London: Burns and Oates).

MORALITY

"A merely casuistic moral theology," writes Josef Pieper, "assumes the immaturity of human beings. Moreover, it intensifies and perpetuates this immaturity." [1] There is probably no aspect of the parish mission which stands in greater need of adaptation to present circumstances than the moral formation it gives its subjects. If one would seek the roots of modern sexual neurosis, for example, one has to look deeper than into books on moral theology. How far, we should ask, is the moral disorder of today associated with modern man's loss of a sense of his historical vocation? Does the fact that he no longer feels an organic sense of belonging to his world and society account for his present mood of escapism? Without going as far as Gustave Thibon, and saying that there are more invalids to cure today than sinners to convert, there are strong grounds for believing that the emotional starvation that man experiences in his working life, in his leisure, and in his home and family, have a great bearing on his views on sexuality, and on the consequences which follow.

"The ethical deeds of man," Pieper continues, "are not more or less fixed manual techniques, whose end is the shaping of some work, but the steps toward self-realization. The human self, which grows toward perfection by accomplishing the good, is a 'work' which surpasses all preconceived blueprints based upon man's own calculations."

With one's ear to the ground today, it is impossible to

[1] Josef Pieper, *Prudence* (New York: Pantheon, 1959).

escape the fact that, for the mass of people, the moral problems emphasized with such regularity from pulpit and press (sexual promiscuity, contraception, and divorce) are problems only for the moralist; the average person does not regard these problems as obstacles in the way of his personal development or self-expression. Some do, of course, accept the rulings of the moralists and follow the natural law and the Ten Commandments, but usually only in so far as they are the law which must be obeyed, otherwise. . . . But the vast majority feel no need for a law which is presented to them less in terms of foundations for building up a truly human life and more in those of prison bars restricting what, in their minds and hearts, stands for human freedom.

In present circumstances, therefore, the teaching mission of the contemporary parish can no longer handle the situation as in the past, when its subjects were sustained by a network of customs and conventions in living, and could get on quite well without having to be continually told the reason for doing what was right. A prudent judgment a parish could make on the contemporary situation would be that truly moral life and action are not possible without maturity. The mission of the parish can, therefore, pursue only one direction, and that is to bring all its subjects through all the various and graduated stages of development to their full maturity as persons made by a personal God and destined by Him to play an irreplaceable and unique rôle in the implementation of His plans for humanity.

3

The Second Longer Look

---

*Point out to me the happy man,
and I will show you selfishness,
egotism, evil—or an abysmal
ignorance.*

GRAHAM GREENE

"Harry," I said to one of the altar boys who had been absent from High Mass, "your first duty is to the parish, not to outside organizations." Harry, a young electrical engineer, had spent his Sunday at a Young Christian Workers' study day; he had sacrificed and sanctified his day of rest to learn how to dedicate the six remaining days of the week to bringing Christ into the lives of his workmates and friends.

I wondered afterwards what had been my motive in reprimanding him—for his sake, or for my own convenience? As his educator in the Church, I had used my authority to tell him that fulfilling his duty as a server was more important than an intensive day's study with other working boys discovering the needs and problems of working youth.

Like many of my fellow priests, I am intensely aware of

the loss to parish life of some of the best type of youth. I visit the local interparochial school regularly, where my own young parishioners are assembled for me and I urge on them the duty of attending Sunday Mass at their own parish church.

While I am there, I notice that the older boys and girls seem slightly bored with what I am saying. Later, over a cup of coffee with the headmaster, he tells me that he, too, has lost the co-operation and interest of those in their last year or two at school and is at a loss to know what to do.

I begin to ask myself: are we muzzling our youth and cramping their natural style with the red tape of petty parochialism? Is youth work in the Church insufficiently geared to the specific contribution youth can make to the life of the Christian community?

I asked Harry to come round to see me and give me his point of view. "Father," he said, "since I've been in the Y.C.W., I've felt that I have discovered a sense of purpose which I never had before in the Church. I feel I belong. Everything in my life now has a greater significance and meaning, especially other people. I have become interested in the lives of the other lads I work with. I notice things I hadn't noticed before: how lonely and isolated is the youngster starting work for the first time, how easy it is for him, unless he is helped, to go with the stream and ape his elders. Most of all I've discovered that our Lord and the Church needs me, that He can't do without me or I without Him. Being a Christian now isn't just a matter of going to Mass every Sunday or doing something extraordinary, like jumping into a river to save a drowning man, but discovering how valuable and meaningful are the everyday actions of my life, for these present me with so many opportunities of serving my fellow workers and showing Christ to them."

The first principle of all missionary action is "to understand and to be understood." I had been in the parish twenty years, had baptized hundreds of the children born there, taught them, and was now beginning to officiate at their marriages. After my conversation with Harry, I had to confess that, despite all my efforts in building schools and running a youth service, I had failed to understand the youth of the parish. It was quite clear, too, that they had failed to understand me. I had been presenting the Church and the Christian way of life to them in a way which did not accord with their basic human needs. They had to go outside the pattern of conventional parish life for these needs to be satisfied.

The parish in its conventional dress was not teaching them adequately the meaning of Christian witness in the twentieth century. On the contrary, it was gagging them. In some ways, it was carrying out a purely administrative rôle in the general life of the Church, existing, as it were, on the fringe of the twentieth-century mission of the Church.

If the parish was to satisfy the aspirations of its members, it was important that it began to understand the society which gave them these aspirations. I thought of Cardinal Mercier's words: that the most important study after the Bible is society. The social life of those living in the parish had changed considerably since I had been appointed to the parish. I had been trying to run a parish as if these changes had never taken place.

One of the few extras I had asked the people to do for the parish was, twice a year, to sell raffle books for the parish lottery. For two or three Sundays before the draw, I had spoken of their responsibility for supporting the building program. Once I remember mentioning how a group of Irish workmen had built an extension to a country parish church during the year they had been engaged on road-making near the parish. Such loyalty should be emulated by my parishioners. But was this type of "building the Church" all that I wanted them to do?

Among my parishioners were a number of bank managers responsible in civic life for the reputation of big banking concerns and for the bank balances of many firms and private depositors. There were managing directors, a doctor or two, foremen, skilled and unskilled working men: all carrying some responsibility in their everyday lives, many family men with great responsibilities in raising a family, a few engaged in trade union or local government work.

I began to shudder at my *gaucherie* in giving these people the selling of raffle tickets as the norm of their commitment in the life of the parish. And what of the other jobs in the parish they took such great delight in carrying out for me: showing people to their seats at Sunday Mass, taking up the collection, putting out the tables for the weekly bingo, sitting on committees to plan the annual garden fête? All adult members of the society in which they lived and worked—and all of them tremendously pleased and honored when I gave them some toy of parish administration to play with for a while!

I began to understand why the parish had come to exist, not only on the outside of the life of local contemporary society, but also on the margin of the contemporary life of the Church. I had made my people so many spiritual Peter Pans. I had been training them, not to live in the twentieth century with all its many complex problems in human living (and the vast new opportunities it presented in Christian witness), but for a situation which no longer existed, that of the preceding century.

The claims we make for the superiority of a Christian education over all others are based on the belief that Christianity's idea for the human person is one corresponding most truly with his nature, in all its originality and with all its capabilities. The educated or mature Christian should be, by rights, the most responsible of men, because he best responds or answers to the challenges to human achievement in the world around him. The truly Catholic Christian is the member of the human race most *present* in his surrounding society, most aware of what is happening around him, most organically active in his environment.

I examined the case histories of a number of my parishioners. There was the town councilor, who was our master of ceremonies at High Mass. He had sat on the local council for many years, was universally admired and respected, could always be relied upon to present the "Catholic case" when necessary and defend the interests of the Catholic community. I could remember no occasion when he had come to me other than to check up on a point of moral theology. He had asked for no spiritual guidance other than what he received as a general member of the parish from the pulpit or in the confessional. His personal sanctification had not kept pace with the rise in his political career. He was a doughty "fighter" for the Church, but I doubt whether any of his non-Catholic friends or political henchmen had ever felt drawn nearer to the Church as their common mother through his social and political activities. I think he had rather scared them off, and they were consequently slightly afraid of the Church.

Then there were the enthusiastic members of the youth club, mostly ex-grammar and convent schoolboys and girls, who had the anti-Communist bee in their bonnets. What they didn't know about Christian apologetics was nobody's business. They carried out a very useful apostolate selling Catholic newspapers outside the railway station and at the bus yard, defending the doctrine of the Church in their offices and workrooms, debating with teams from other youth groups in the locality. To put Christ back into Christmas meant for them promoting sales of Christian Christmas cards or arranging for cribs to be displayed in theater foyers. One admired their zeal and loyalty. But was this the only missionary action needed in the contemporary situation? What if its overindulgence was preventing them from carrying out Christian action at a deeper level? None had ever come to me other than for permission to inaugurate some project or to check up on some point of apologetics or morality. Again, their personal sanctification was geared to notions of the Church imbibed at school which were now serving as a kind of spiritual strait jacket hindering their maturation.

I have sometimes heard old parishioners say that things were much better in the past when we had to fight for our Faith. I wonder if anybody but an English Catholic could make such remarks, as though one preferred the lack of opportunities of the past to the effort of uncovering the immense opportunities of the present.

"We have a very rich past," said Archbishop Montini at the first World Congress of the Lay Apostolate in 1951, "so that we are sometimes inclined to think that all has been done." Such a viewpoint has no place in the modern missionary conception of the parish. We are, as it were, at the beginning once again, as though nothing had ever been done. The task of every parish is to lay the foundation stone of the Christian reality of tomorrow. To inaugurate such a feast of charity calls for new methods in the parish apostolate.

These new missionary methods mean a complete break with the former Catholic ghettoism. They must aim at giving each member of the parish the Christian training and formation fitting him for an historical vocation in his contemporary society. If the parish is to carry out an organically missionary rôle in local society, her organic life must be strengthened and enriched. This means that each of the members who make up her living body or organism must be given a true vision of why they are vital to the life of the Church. Each must be weaned from a narrow view of that membership which confines them to merely an organizational rôle in the Church.

I went into the waiting room and there met a middle-aged man who asked for instructions in the Faith. "For years," he said, "I have fought the Roman Catholic Church and all organized religion as a member of the Communist Party. On our local trades council were two other Communists as well as myself, a lapsed Catholic and a practicing one. The practicing one was always fighting us on matters on which the Church held differing views, but he never gave the impression that he was fighting to uphold his Church. He had a tremendous reverence and respect for his fellow men, and where he chose to disagree with us he was doing so to uphold their essential rights and dignity as human beings. He was a first-class trade unionist because he was a first-class Christian. He wasn't out for personal ambition or power, and he wasn't out to get more influence and power for his Church. He was a man of complete integrity. Although we had plenty of battles over the table, we all knew that he would be the first man we would go to in any personal trouble—as we did. He had our fullest confidence and trust. He has brought me to the Catholic Church because of his tremendous sense of commitment, and I would like to serve under the same flag of personal freedom and justice."

An authentic missionary parish capable of becoming the vital principle of unity in local society is built up, not primarily on organization or techniques in presenting Christian truth, but on personal contact. The most powerful impact we know is that of one person upon another. The richer the personal qualities, the deeper the level of personal life, the greater the impact of one person upon another.

Our parishes have up to now concentrated on perfecting their organizational life. The time has come to exploit this highly-geared organization in the true interests of its living members. The more alive the members become to their presence as the animators of their surrounding society, the more will the parish carry out its organic, missionary, and collaborative rôle in society, not primarily to make all within its bounds juridical or canonical members of the visible Church, but to bring each to his full stature as a human person according to the Christian ideal.

· 4 ·

A Vital Dimension in Parish Life

*Leave thy country behind thee,
and come away into a land I will
show thee. Then I will make a
great people of thee.*
GOD'S PROMISE TO ABRAHAM

"More like an English summer," is the usual comment when
Cardinal Newman's sermon on the Second Spring of English Catholicism is mentioned. At first sight, this view may
seem to be justified. English Catholics are still in the minor-
ity and not apparently having much effect on the life of a nation which over the last century has become progressively
more godless and materialistic. Was, then, Newman less of a
prophet than his reputations and writings would make it
appear? Or did some obstacle come in the way of what he
felt was inevitable once the hierarchy was re-established in
England?

If Newman was the visionary and strategist, Cardinal
Manning, his contemporary, was the tactician. Together
they might have made the Second Spring an actuality;
since they did not, it would appear that the lines on which

the battle for England's soul was fought from that time to this have taken a wrong direction. Or, might we say, that the lines were never sufficiently grasped and have ever since been buried in the archives awaiting a deeper appraisal and recognition?

It is an indication of the attitude adopted by some parishes that the word *universal*, when applied to the Church, is commonly accepted as meaning *widespread*, as though the fact that the Church is spread all over the world accounts for her claim to be the Universal Church. Perhaps this also accounts for the fact that over the last fifty years the average English Catholic has taken much pride (one might say most pride) in outside compliments which placed the Church on a par with the Imperial German Army and the Standard Oil Company as one of the three greatest organizations in the world, and Catholicism on a par with Communism and Fascism as one of the three most powerful ideologies.

The notion of "universal" means something far more than being widespread. Indeed, it means something almost the contrary—the bringing back of what is widespread or diverse into an already existing oneness, as can be seen by examining the derivation of the word—uni-versal.

Yves Congar puts labels on these two rival definitions of universal or Catholic. One he calls quantitative or geographical; the other, qualitative or innate. He also states:

There cannot be quantitative catholicity without qualitative, the latter being the necessary cause of the former. If the Church is indeed able and destined to extend over the world, it is in virtue of the universal assimilative capacity of her constituent principles. The catholicity of the Church, regarded as a property of her being, is the dynamic universality of her principles of unity to assimilate, fulfill, and raise to God in oneness with him, all men and every man and every human value.[1]

To pass from a sense of the Church's quantitative catholicity to the qualitative is a kind of graduation in the Church's school of Christian formation. One thereby arrives at a new, higher stage of one's maturation. The earlier, slightly jingoistic Catholic becomes the authentic missionary member of the Church. No longer does one evaluate success for the Church in terms of numbers or territory, but in those of assimilation.

The mystery of the Church's mission to the world remains a mystery, as it always must, so long as one does not over-rationalize it, or imagine that we know all there is to know about it. The Church for us on earth can never be more than the beginning of our joy, since we are always on the threshold of discovering her, as it were, for the first time: unfathomable are her riches and mysterious her ways. Christ constantly speaks of His Kingdom as a mystery. Like other mysteries of the Faith, this can be "solved" only in the form of a vital act whereby each member of the Kingdom elects to receive it as a gift and to share it.[2]

The danger always facing a Christian is the temptation

[1] Yves M.J. Congar, O.P., *Divided Christendom* (Centenary Press, 1939).
[2] Romano Guardini, *Faith and Modern Man* (New York: Pantheon, 1952).

to receive this gift of God, not on God's terms, but on his own: to lay down our own conditions for receiving a divine gift, to usurp the Kingdom, to de-mystify it, and make it conform to our own limited and self-sufficient standards. English Catholicism in parish life has not always managed to resist this temptation, as is shown only too clearly by its failure to become conscious of the need to support the rest of the Church and particularly the mission in Africa, Asia, and South America.

A truly "foreign-missionary" conscience has never been formed in the ranks of average members of the parish, priest and layman, because the work of the foreign missions has been regarded as an expression of the Church's quantitative catholicity. That English parish life has come, therefore, to be self-sufficient in itself, living in a self-contained watertight compartment, and depriving itself of the enrichment to its organic life which would arise from a deep love of the foreign missionary apostolate of the Church, is conclusive proof that the standard of average parish spirituality has never graduated to Christian maturity.

We can also identify in this "parochialism" the reason why the average Catholic Christian appears to find himself unable to define the missionary character of the Church (and of his parish) as something organic in the life of his local society, since the word is associated by him with the "foreign missions," and this, to him, has always seemed to be a part-time Cinderella activity of the Church. This restriction withholds from him the vital missionary character of every parish in the Church. Catholic and missionary never become for him synonymous. For him, also, Catholic life loses its underlying unity, for the Church becomes divided in itself, carrying on two separated apostolates. Furthermore, he can see the Church only in terms of her institution, like a Colossus striding the world, and never establishes contact with her continual organic development.

It is not the normal habit of the average Catholic parishioner to think of parish life as something in a state of continual maturation or growth, but more in terms of brick-and-mortar extension. This is probably why Pierre Maillaud can say of English Catholic life during the last hundred years "that its position is not discussed here because, however powerful its influence in the past or its potential influence in the future, it does not at present penetrate the social consciousness or act upon the national way of life." [1]

"Only when old Asiatic cultures have found their place in the Christian order," once wrote a French Jesuit anthropologist who had spent a lifetime in China, "will the expression of Christianity be complete." Père Danielou makes a similar point: "Up to now Christianity has been refracted only through the Greek and Roman worlds; it still remains to be refracted through the Chinese and Hindu facets in order to find fulfillment at the end of time, when not only every individual but every civilization will have been christianized." These statements are mentioned to pose a question. Are such sentiments or such a wide vision of the Church part of the normal Catholic mentality of the average member of an English Catholic parish? The answer

[1] Pierre Maillaud, *The English Way* (New York: Oxford University Press).

would give some indication of the state of spiritual maturity in such a parish today.

There are, however, grounds for thinking that such a mentality was envisaged as the norm even so far back as the restoration of the English Catholic hierarchy. The young Father Herbert Vaughan, later to found the English Foreign Missionary Society at Mill Hill, found Cardinal Wiseman particularly enthusiastic about his ideals. Cardinal Manning, too, recognized the importance of the foreign missionary apostolate and was not slow to give it primacy of place. Despite the ever-growing needs of the Catholic body of the nineteenth century—churches, schools, orphanages, organizations—he made it quite clear that the first, overriding obligation of English Catholics was, not to themselves, but to the foreign missions. A study of the policies of his successors in the primatial See of Westminster shows that each was aware that the foreign missionary apostolate had something of great value to give to English Catholic life, was the most effective way of bringing about the conversion of England to the true Faith, that if the seed of this apostolic love was carefully watered and cultivated it could in time compensate for the apostasy of the clergy and laity in the sixteenth century.

There are also grounds for thinking that the lines of direction English Catholic life was intended to take over the last century were recognized, but came to be buried in the archives. Deeply hidden beneath the vast efforts which have been made for the Catholic cause in England, in both past and present, can be heard a constantly nagging voice of conscience: a good deal of this effort produces only phantom fruit. It is a voice which today is becoming increasingly articulate as English Catholics see the original peoples of the British Empire and the Commonwealth of Nations coming of age.

Today it is becoming gradually recognized that the hinge on which the universal apostolate of the Church will hang in the balance for some considerable time is the work of putting the peoples of the under-developed countries on their feet.[1] The position England holds in Africa and Asia eminently fits English Catholics for a key rôle in the immense work of racial co-operation. English Catholics have in these times received a challenge seldom given to any nation or people in the history of the Church, one which, if answered, would revitalize Catholic life at home and possibly make this century the greatest in its history.

"Our great concern in the West," writes Lance Wright, "is how to form a new ideal of lay life, of a life which will unmistakably be a life of sacrifice, but which will equally be a life spent in the world, using the liberties proper to a life in the world. Because of the failure to launch such an ideal our people are compelled to model themselves on those they see about them. Each year our schools turn out a fresh harvest of school-leavers full of generosity and enthusiasm, and we know that these qualities are going to run to waste. If only, we feel, that they could have a genuine experience of Christian life before it is too late. One could conceive of a vast effort by the Catholics of the old industrialized countries to put their experience and their technical skills at the service of those nations which are just entering

[1] *Laymen Face the World:* Volume II of Report on Second World Congress for the Lay Apostolate (Rome: Permanent Committee for International Congresses of the Lay Apostolate).

the modern world, of it becoming almost the normal thing for Catholic young men and women to spend the first two years after completing their professional training by practicing their skills in the Missions. If really large numbers were to do something like this, how much easier it would be for people to see the reality of the Church and how greatly would our concept of the layman's life be enriched. Asia and Africa offer supreme opportunities for re-Christianizing the life of the laity in Europe and North America." [1]

Recently one has read of how, when three young Belgian workers were killed in an air crash while on their way to join a team of lay apostles in Africa, twenty other young men in Belgium volunteered immediately to take their places. Is it criticizing English Catholic life and education too harshly to mention that such apostolic zeal could not, at its present stage of development, find any parallel among our Catholic youth? There are isolated English Catholic young men who have given up their homes and work, to live among the African youth, Kevin Muir of the Y.C.W. for one, but as demands for others increase day by day, there is scarcely any response. When, for example, ten non-British Europeans are refused visas to enter India to work in the lay apostolate and it is known that these visas will be given only to people of British nationality, vital work for the Church is left undone because ten young British Catholics are not available. They would be available, not in their tens, but in their hundreds, if vital stages in their maturation as Catholic Christians had not been left out,

[1] *Ibid.*

and if a foreign missionary conscience had in the process become a natural part of their Catholic spirituality.

Why, we may ask, therefore, have the directives and intentions of the Catholic hierarchy over the last century never been sufficiently followed by the English Catholic community? Perhaps the reasons are as much psychological as theological. The Englishman (and the English Catholic has as yet never been able to fuse his Englishness with his Catholicism) is usually a victim of the "watertight compartment" mind. He also believes that man-made organization is a cure for all organic ills and tends to forget that the cause and effect of most organization is to build a barrier between oneself and the rest of the world. Both traits are endemic to English Catholic life, as the history of the Catholic Schools Question in England shows. (Only in our own time are we recognizing that the Catholic school is subordinate to the Christian community, and that its primary importance is not to defend the rights of parents or children, but to keep alive the idea of Christian education in a secularized society.)

But if there are psychological reasons for explaining the absence of a vital dimension in English Catholic life, it is rather with the priest as the educator of consciences that one will find the deeper underlying cause of a lack of a missionary consciousness in English Catholics. This lack of a sense of mission, recognizable not only in irresponsibility for the missions but also in the ineffectiveness of the vast majority of good practicing Catholics in their own national life, must inevitably be traced to the type of for-

mation or lack of proper formation given to the laity by
its priests.

To say this does not necessarily mean that the vast majority of priests will agree. Indeed, before one can analyze
the lack of a missionary conscience, one has to face the fact
that for many this lack is not usually accepted as a lack,
or if a lack, of little consequence in the making of the
Church in England. Very few treat the foreign missions as
anything other than a work of supererogation, of little consequence in the running of a parish or Catholic organization.
Fewer would associate the indifference, the misguided zeal,
the lapsation, the resistance to the supernatural we meet all
over the parish, let alone the lack of unity in marriage and
the breakdown in family life, with the absence of a foreign
missionary conscience in the people.

There are, of course, individual priests who have discovered after long periods of trial and error that a parish
grows and flourishes the more foreign-missionary-minded
the parishioners become: some, indeed, who have found the
foreign missions more financially successful than football
pools; but these are so rare that their individual witness
can be regarded as non-existent.

The question really to be answered is who is right: the
priest who is benevolently neutral to the foreign missions
or the one who makes this apostolate an integral part of his
parish administration?

A common ground for a discussion on this point is, as
it can only be, the origin and end of all parish life: the individual person living in community. The parish exists to
bring the life of God to all within its boundaries. The erec-

tion of churches and schools, the forming of societies and organizations, the administration of the sacraments, the celebration of Mass, the preaching of the Gospel, have only one end: to enable every person for whom the parish priest is responsible to begin living a new mode of existence —the divine.

Can, therefore, they live such a life without a foreign missionary conscience? To answer this question, we need to dig still further and examine with some science and precision the type of spirituality the diocesan clergy must aim at giving their flocks. And to do this, it is first of all necessary to find out, with as much exactitude, what the spirituality is that the diocesan clergy themselves aspire to.

For over thirty years, since Pope Pius XI revived foreign missionary zeal as "the first burning purpose of Christ," parochial life in the Church has had at hand a powerful means of revitalizing itself. The average parish has failed to exploit this valuable weapon. The reasons for this failure are many and diverse. Some have been already mentioned; these stem from an inadequate knowledge of the mystery of the Church. Others, which concern a lack of experience in the presentation of the foreign missions, also need to be considered.

These are not unconnected with the general spiritual arrestment endemic to average Catholic life. A foreign missionary conscience is formed in children who attend Catholic schools, and is then allowed to run to seed. In much the same way as Catholics carry on into adult life the half-formed attitudes toward the Faith they acquired at school, so, too, their sense of responsibility for the foreign missionary apostolate seldom leaves the stage it reached in the classroom. Holy Childhood Day becomes Mission Sunday, but is celebrated as a kind of Church "Empire Day" when time is snatched from more pressing attachments in the parish to pay tribute to the "lone" missionary in foreign lands.

Pope Pius XI was at pains to defend Mission Sunday from any association with the collecting box. As the Pope of Catholic Action, he saw that in this matter of mission aid the changing status of the laity must be taken into account. The "romantic" presentation of the foreign missions given in the classroom could retard the full development of a missionary conscience unless it was adapted to the greater maturity of the adult Catholic. The clergy were urged by him to present the foreign missionary apostolate as "the daily concern" of every member of the Church, and as an integral part of her total apostolate.

Much of the propaganda used to spread foreign missionary zeal has conformed to a set pattern in which vivid personal pictures of the missioner at work, statistics, and emphasis on the bizarre and exotic in foreign lands have predominated. It has always been a fairly successful method and one not to be scoffed at, but this pictorial presentation can appeal only to a certain type of Catholic and touches only superficially on the real issues involved in the universal mission of the Church. A more realistic approach, particularly from the doctrinal or theological standpoint, is necessary if this work is to be recognized by the rank and file of the Church as part of the Church's program to reinform contemporary society with a full idea of her personality.

"The most providential and most notable movement within Christian society today is a return to contemplation and study of the mystery of the Church," writes Père Congar. Interest in the foreign missions as one of the main movements through which the Church is revealing her mystery, therefore, needs to be presented in a way through which the average member of the Church will deepen and enrich his knowledge of the Church and her mission to contemporary society.

Again, while admitting that it is necessary for foreign missionary societies to appeal from pulpit and press to finance their work in pagan lands, this type of propaganda should not be seen as the only effective way of educating the average Catholic in his missionary responsibilities. The foreign missions have suffered too much in the past from being financed from the sales of used stamps and sales-tax stamps. They are more than a poor relation in the Christian family.

During the last half-century, particularly, they have served the Church as a living laboratory. "Missionary activity," wrote the late Cardinal van Rossum, "in all its forms is so important that it must be called vital, for with it the Church lives; without it she dies. Through it we can actually intensify the life and fruitfulness of our universal Mother."

One might truly say that the modern lay apostolate was born out of the missionary method employed by Pope Pius XI in Africa, that Cardijn's Young Christian Workers first saw the light of day in missionary research carried out among the native cultures of Uganda and the Congo, that the liturgical renaissance was fed on the experiments carried out all over the missionary world to make the sacramental life of the Church assimilable to pagan peoples.

If long-established Christian countries like Spain, France, and Ireland have given much support to the missionary countries over the years, this should not blind one to the fact that the missionary countries have amply repaid the debt by working out in the concrete, for the benefit of the whole Church, a true picture of the mystery of adaptation. To a great extent this central mystery of Christianity had lost much of its impetus in Catholic life in the long-established Christian countries. That it has been rediscovered in our own times is due in the main to the many experiments in adapting a divine principle of life to a variegated human condition that have been carried out in the missionary countries.

Were this sufficiently realized, the norm of mission-aid given by the average Catholic parish in Europe and America would change considerably. Home and foreign missionary work would be more clearly seen as two sides of the same coin. Efforts would assuredly be made to bring students and workers arriving from the under-developed countries into the life of a parish. Steps would be taken to establish some kind of personal relationship between parishes and mission stations, seminaries at home and seminaries in the mission fields.

To a great extent, present-day techniques and methods of interesting people in the work of the foreign missions are out of touch with actuality. More is at stake in this matter of mission aid and interest than the horizontal spread of the Church through the acquirement of property and buildings. As the tragedy of the Church in China witnessed, Christianity must become organically present in the lives and thought of the people in missionary territories. Members of the Church in her totality need to be brought to a stage of enlightened interest and participation in her universal mission. Unless the real problems facing the Church in this mission to mankind are identified and understood by the rank and file of her members in every parish, many of the opportunities given her in these times of world crisis and world unification of becoming in the concrete the vital principle of unity in contemporary society, would be lost.

Perhaps we can now better answer whether a love of the foreign missionary apostolate is something essential in the apostolate and, therefore, in the spirituality of the diocesan priest. If his mission is to serve the community of persons, then this service of education or nourishment cannot fall short of eventually bringing each person to a full, living membership in the Church—and this means a total involvement in her total apostolate.

To restrict the apostolic action of his parishioners to the confines of the parish or nation is to deny them the exercise of a love which is the essence of their new mode of existence as members of the Church. By rights they should be bringing to their parish a love which is the love of the whole Church; instead, they love it with a love turned in on itself. No parish can survive such treatment, nor can its members. They are left with a spirituality which, because it is less than that of a member of the Church, condemns them to immaturity and mediocrity in the life of the parish.

On a national scale, the extent of this spiritual immaturity becomes a menace. The Church becomes continually misrepresented as a self-enclosed group active only in the interests of sectarian advantage or ecclesiastical privilege, as a world-wide organization continually seeking new victims to increase her power, as a powerful ideology preaching a vague anti-Communism. Her essential work of animation in an already-existing society lacks fire because her members, deprived of a total view of the Church, cannot bring to the organic life of the Church an action which is effective (in assimilating, raising up, and restoring back in unity with God every human person and value in the parish) only because it shares with the Church her divine mode of operation.

If today, then, in England we feel that the mature lay apostolate has got off to a late start, that despite all the encouraging returns in the annual census of the Church we are in much the same position as we were a century ago, that Papal directives to the laity to come to the assistance of the missions are unheeded and unanswered, an examination in depth into the state of English Catholicism might show that its weakness is in the last analysis that of starvation due to cutting ourselves away from the only life line which would have brought us into the full life of the Church—her foreign missionary apostolate, the source of her continual fertility and growth. The Second Spring will come, not through increases in numbers, better techniques, or more efficient organization, but through men and women of faith who have been given by the diocesan clergy a spirituality consistent with their mission in the Church, a genuinely Catholic, i.e., missionary, spirituality.

We are said to be entering the third great missionary era in the history of the Church, and to be at the end of an age in which the missions had their own distinct existence in the Church. Pope Pius XII not only spoke continuously of this new missionary era, but inaugurated it in the first year of his pontificate, with a gesture the significance of which is only fully grasped when it is placed alongside Pope Pius XI's consecration in Rome of the six Chinese bishops in 1926. Pius XII's twelve bishops, consecrated in St. Peter's in 1939, were truly representative "of peoples or groups of peoples of the most varied kind." He was in fact inaugurating a missionary era in the Church built up on the belief that the erstwhile foreign missionary countries had now graduated to a *normal* existence in the Church. These countries and nations were no longer on the receiving end of the Church's universal apostolate; they were ready to make their own unique contribution to the common supernatural life of the Church. "As Christ assumed a real human nature, so the Church likewise," said Pius XII, "assumes the fullness of all that is authentically human, and by elevating it makes it a source of supernatural power in whatever place and under whatever form she finds it."

The new missionary era of the Church, therefore, differs from others in that it seeks to make the Church *organically* universal, and this for the first time in its history. We are now entering an age of exchange in the Church. The word *universal* is now becoming understood in its purest sense.

No longer can the missionary work of the Church be interpreted as "a spreading outwards." Now it must be seen as "a gathering together," a bringing together, a natural turning of mankind in all its richly variegated hues and along all its labyrinthine ways to discover its completion in the *Totus Christus*, Christ's Social Body. It must be viewed as the gathering together in oneness, the raising up and restoring back into unity with God every human person and every human value.

Pius XII spoke of the deep meaning of the Church's vital law of adaptation as a tireless and gentle following of the providential road of time and circumstance. She cannot be a foreigner in any place or at any time. Every country contributes to her life and development. But her presence at the very heart of human history is an exchange of life and energy. She receives whatever is authentically human and breathes into it her own divine principle of life. She effects a mysterious synthesis of the divine and human, the natural and the supernatural. She adapts an unchangeable divine mode of life to an ever-changing human situation.

As the Church sees it, she is at the opening of a new feast of charity. The late Holy Father urged the faithful to become aware of their commitment in the present opportunities by regearing their charity to this new stage in the missionary history of the Church. No longer taking oneself as a model in judging others, he said, open your minds sincerely and wide in an effort to understand, to esteem, and to love them.

The Relevance of Hope in a Parish

*How differently the Apocalypse
affects us from the predictions
of Isaias.*

CARDINAL NEWMAN

Whenever one sees the essential organic growth of the
parish community being sacrificed on the altar of external
ecclesiastical organization, it is time to examine what kind
of hope directs the action of the parish.

The one thing hoped for in a machine is that it will not
break down. From the moment a machine takes shape on
the drawing board until it leaves the workshop or assembly
line, it is already something complete in itself. Should one
of its parts reveal a flaw in its workmanship, there is always
a spare to take its place.

With a living reality, however, the position is very
different. Here hope transcends both optimism and pessimism. "It is neither comprehension and possession nor
simply non-possession, but not-yet-possession." A living

reality rises or declines in vigor and virility according to
the rate of maturation of its constituent elements. It is not
ready-made, but in a state of continual development. Hope
rests in the belief that whatever is organic or living will,
in passing through its various stages of growth, eventually
attain the fullness of its own truth and goodness.

Applying this distinction between a machine and a living
reality to the parish, an overstress on the organization-
parish at the expense of the organism-parish takes away
most of the relevance of the theological gift of hope in its
mission. Once the justification of a parish is confined to a
faultless carrying out of its regulative functions, a sense of
the Church as a people on the move no longer gives the
parish an eschatological bearing.

That devotion to Christ as King of Kings and Lord of
Lords has been singularly marked out by the divine Will
to be the supreme guide in repairing the spiritual and social
disintegration of our times is evident in three significant
gestures by recent Popes. In the dying days of the last
century, Leo XIII consecrated the human race to the Sacred
Heart of Jesus. As the needs of the new century became
more defined, Pius XI instituted a new liturgical feast of
the Kingship of Christ. In the first encyclical of his pontificate, Pius XII indicated that the cult of the Divine Heart
of Christ was to be its whole inspiration and guiding light.

There is no doubt that the new impetus given by modern
Popes to this devotion has brought about a transformation
in Catholic-Christian thought and action. Many have found
in it a deeper awareness of their membership of the Church,

have acquired a genuinely missionary or Catholic conscience, have found in their hearts a renewed feeling of
human solidarity and kinship.

Such signs of a greater spiritual maturity are themselves
proof that there is reviving in the modern Church a virtue
without which the mystery of the Kingdom of Christ
would be inconceivable, and with which it must always be
closely associated. Of the three divine energies implanted
in the human person at baptism, that of hope is most closely
connected with Christian maturity; for whereas faith tells
us of God's creative and redemptive plans, hope is the
divine invitation to enter into these plans, as co-worker
and co-redeemer, and as a member of a kingdom which
has no spare parts.

Innate in the mystery of the Kingdom, writes Père
Congar, is the divine will that what has been done once and
for all in Christ, the royal priest, may be done by everyone,
that his mystery should become theirs, his passing their
passing, and his sitting at the right hand of the Father their
sitting as children of God and co-heirs with Christ.

The mission which the Holy Ghost carries out in the
Church is one that complements that of the Son of God.
In making each child of God his temple, the Holy Ghost
fashions each to become a living, breathing stone of the
Church, God's Temple. The mission of the Holy Ghost
cannot fail to respect both the original elements of each
inviolable human person and the actual circumstances in
which each person is willed by God to live his life on this
earth. There are no press buttons, no supernaturalism, in

the Kingdom of God on earth. It is a work of continual development and maturation through which each member of the Church is led through all the stages of growth, making at each that contribution to the organic life of the Kingdom necessary if it is to be realized in the concrete of time and place, until it reaches its plenitude at the end of time.

The theological virtue of hope is a gift of God enabling the Christian to live for the future, but in the present. The certain knowledge that his Lord and Master will return at the end of time colors all his thoughts and deeds. It energizes, transforms, and rejuvenates his whole being. He is, indeed, one who waits, but also one for whom everything in life is caught up in the urgency and joyfulness of a future event. For the Christian the whole sense of time has changed.

For the Christian energized by hope, the here-and-the-now is no mere filling in of time, but a filling of time with God. Hope, with its lightness and buoyancy, induces in him a readiness for action. There is no evasion of reality for him. All things must be restored to Christ, Lord of Lords and King of Kings. His times and his situation must be ready at the end of time, when Christ returns to receive a kingdom already won, to enter their glory as part of that kingdom. As a member of that Kingdom, he has providentially been set down at a certain time in human history and in a certain location to exercise the art of the Christian priesthood and, in, through, and by Christ, to impregnate them with the peace and justice of God.

There is in our Lord's parables of the Kingdom a warning that it is not hope, but a false optimism or pessimism, when members of the Kingdom refuse to enter it on God's terms as a gift, but on their own.

The optimists would condemn the Church to the existence of a lifeless corpse, imagining there to be a short cut between the space which separates the ascension of Christ from His return at the end of time, and allowing their own times and civilization to proceed as though God were absent in the affairs of men and no longer the Lord of History.

The pessimists, who are the other side of the coin, remain as refugees within the situation, dissatisfied, disheartened, or indifferent, refusing to use their abilities and powers to further the interests of the Kingdom by becoming more present as Christians in the life of their time and country.

Both are contrary to a belief in the Kingdom as one *in via*, on its way, to the end of time. Both resist what is integral to this Kingdom—the truth that Christianity has put up the price of everything in the market of values and that now everything has an infinite price.

This age of Christ the King has blazoned forth also as the age of the rediscovery of the dignity and value of the human person. Hope has returned to contemporary mankind in a cult which re-establishes each individual person as someone needed by God for the fulfilment of His plans. In truth, Christ's Kingdom is the Kingdom of no spare parts for, in the realization of that kingdom, no one is expendable; all have something unique to contribute of their lives and of their times. No one can doubt the providence of this in times when men everywhere are avoiding life, living a new form of existence with freedom at zero, glorying in the cult of failure, and demanding only "the capacity to face despair."

If the average member of a parish is to be sustained by a genuine Christian hope and is not to take refuge behind its parody, the life of a parish can never be restricted to a merely organizational or administrative existence. This way lies that of a spiritual proletariat. It must not contain the people forever in a spiritual "Peter Pan-hood." They must be taken through all the natural stages of personal development as members of the Church, with their sights continually raised to take in a vision of the whole world. The modern Christian must be directed to become the most engaged man of his generation. He is responsible for his generation. He must become the one most present in the life of his times. Christian hope makes this demand on him as a member of a kingdom *in via*.

In the absence of this hope, his policy will remain one of self-containment and spiritual atrophy. There is much evidence to suggest that a genuine Christian hope needs to be revived in average parish life. Most young people who leave the Church do so through boredom or ennui. The challenge offered them in parish life is one merely of carrying out certain rules and obligations in matters of practice and doctrine. Older people see the Christian ideal less in terms of living their ordinary lives on a divine level of existence and more in those of saving their soul or remaining in a state of grace. For the clergy, stolidity and stagnation masquerade as solidity and stability. The extreme conservatism and mediocrity of much parish life is never identified with a failure in maturation. A loss of a proper sense of direction in its organic mission to contemporary society is covered over by a deceptive security arising from a limited vision.

"The mentality of the Bible," writes Father Charlier, "is one of challenge, one which demands commitment; and it is necessary to get inside that mentality." For genuine Christian hope to revive in a parish and for a sense of itself as a people on the move to become again its whole inspiration and guidance, a return to a biblical presentation of Christian truth is necessary.

Most Catholics who have passed through Catholic schools know a certain number of texts from the Bible by heart. These are learned in much the same way as multiplication tables, as formulae to prove certain erstwhile "controversial" doctrines of the Church. The Scriptures among English Catholics have become to some extent no more than apologetic props to support such doctrines as the infallibility of the Pope, the resurrection of Christ, the Virgin Birth.

Again, so much time has had to be spent in recent years proving, against the rationalists and Higher Critics of the Bible, its inerrancy and inspired character that it has tended to become valued more as a priceless manuscript than as a revelation and recording of God's continual intervention in the history of the world.

We need, therefore, to be reminded by Romano Guardini that revelation is more than the disclosure of certain truths which God wishes mankind to know—it is history. "What God imparted to Abraham," he writes, "was not any illumination concerning His own divine being, or the soul of man, or the nature of eternal salvation and the way to attain it, but the promise to him and to his wife of a son whose descendants would in time become a people. The word of Revelation took the form of 'Come, go with me, act with me'; and the response, the word of faith: 'I am ready to go.'"

The notions of "a kingly people," "a royal priesthood," are ones with deep roots in biblical history. The history of God's intervention in the affairs of man took a new turn with the mission of His Son to this earth. So, too, did the divine invitation to mankind to understand and to take part in divine activity. To be a member of the Church includes all it meant to His chosen people in the Old Testament. For Christians, it is a call to enter a kingdom already one, to live an eternal victory, not only in the hereafter, but in the here-and-now, to celebrate at each moment in time the victory over sin and death, to play an irreplaceable, unique, and historical role in bringing that victory to bear today.

"We have been accustomed," continues Romano Guardini, "to think of the Faith as something systematized, somewhat like the systematizations of knowledge and natural science, or insights into the being of God and the nature of the cosmos. But in the earliest times, Faith was felt to be instruction in the activity of God and a call to understand and take part in it."

Christian hope, therefore, has its historical setting. The

mission of the parish, which, in its essence, is to form man in his fullness, has always and continually been to bring its subjects to that degree of Christian maturity in which they will recognize themselves as a people journeying toward a city and carrying with them on that journey the responsibility of witnessing to their times and to their contemporaries the wonderful works of God. Such a parish organism has a sense of movement, of direction, of development.

"When religious vitality is on the wane," said Cardinal Suhard, "religious life concerns itself with acts of devotion. Conversely, when it is mounting, it spreads from acts of devotion into all the activities of the Christian, even to those which seem most profane."

.6.

The Missionary Method of the Church

> *The very foundation and heart of Christianity is the insertion of the eternal into the temporal, the temporal into the eternal.*
>
> CHARLES PÉGUY

"We have behind us a very rich past," said Cardinal Montini, at the first World Lay Apostolate Congress in 1951, "the wisdom of the Pontiffs, the holiness of those who have built the edifice of the Church, the wealth of Revelation itself and of Tradition, so that one is tempted sometimes to think that everything has been done already and to remain inactive. When, however, we consider present necessities, we are obliged to recognize that we are still at the beginning of things, just as if nothing had been done."

These present necessities demand a new flowering of humanity. Person, family, and community need to rise to new heights of human existence. The new technological era demands an age in which each discovers new forms. Unless personal, family, and community life, as living organisms, identify the problems or obstacles to their continual development and growth present in contemporary society, and find within themselves fresh stores of strength and fertility to overcome the challenge of this new technological age to their inviolability, the crisis through which humanity is passing at the moment, amid so much scientific discovery and technical advance, will leave the person, the family, and the community in an even greater state of disintegration than they are at present.

This crisis facing humanity is, as the late Cardinal Suhard of Paris identified it, a crisis of growth. The problems present in our modern, complex, and highly industrialized way of life are so many new opportunities for human nature to realize in the concrete potentialities hitherto latent and to arrive at a new stage in its continual maturation.

What Cardinal Newman wrote about the development of doctrine applies equally to the growth of the human organism:

When an idea is said to have life, it is not received passively in this or that form in many minds, but it becomes an active principle within them, leading them to an ever-new contemplation of itself, to an application of it in various directions, and a propagation of it on every side. First, there is a general agitation of thought, then a time of confusion when conceptions and misconceptions are in conflict. After a while some definite teaching emerges and this will be surveyed in its relation to other doctrines or facts, interrogated and criticized by enemies, defended by well-wishers. In proporation to its native vigor, the idea will introduce itself into the framework of social life, change public opinion, strengthen or undermine the established order, finally grow into an ethical code.[1]

And as the maturation or germination of an idea on a large mental field cannot progress without cutting across and thereby destroying or modifying and incorporating with itself existing modes of thought and action, so, too, the maturation of the human organism does not take place in isolation, but in continuity and sovereignty, amid the busy scene of contemporary life, adapting itself continually to circumstances of time and place, and seeking its constant fulfillment in the very heart of the human struggle.

Newman continues:

It is elicited and expanded by trial, and battles into perfection and supremacy. In time it enters upon strange territory, points of contact alter their bearing, parties rise and fall around it, dangers and hopes appear in new relations, and old principles reappear under new forms. It changes with them in order to remain the same. In a higher world it is otherwise, but here down below to live is to change, and to be perfect is to have changed often.[2]

Newman, in his essay, puts forward two arguments, one from the rational viewpoint, the other from the historical, to show that developments in Christian doctrine are both to be expected and have actually taken place. Why, we may ask, was he taking such great pains to make his point? Christianity was beginning to face a new attack, not this

[1] John Henry Newman, *An Essay on the Development of Christian Doctrine* (New York: Doubleday, Image Books, 1960).
[2] *Ibid.*

time on some individual doctrine, but on the very basis of its claim to be an historical reality. "Already on the scene," writes Philip Hughes, "were those who openly planned and worked for a new non-religious century, and this in novels and poems as well as in treatises of natural science and social philosophy." [1] The new climate of thought was one denying that religion could ever be *res publica*.

Newman was eager to show that apparent alterations and inconsistencies in Christian doctrine and worship were not evidence of corruption, but signs of a visible growth which has persevered up to the present time without any sign of its coming to an end.

From the nature of the human mind, time is necessary for the full comprehension and perfection of great ideas; the highest and the most wonderful truths, though communicated to the world once for all by inspired teachers, could not be comprehended all at once by the recipients but, as being received and transmitted by minds not inspired and through media which were human, have required only the longer time and deeper thought for their full elucidation. [2]

In retrospect, it can now be seen that Newman was at work pioneering a return to what can be termed a rediscovery of the Church's essential mystery of adaptation. From his day till now, this central mystery of Christianity has never ceased to exercise the mind of the Church; and all the new modern movements through which she is seek-

[1] Msgr. Philip Hughes, *English Catholics* (London: Burns and Oates).
[2] John Henry Newman, *op. cit.*

ing to reveal her personality to the contemporary world, if they are to be rightly appreciated, need to be seen in this context. In speaking, therefore, of the missionary method which she wishes to see employed at every level of Catholic life to fulfill her end and purpose as the Bride of Christ, the implication is that the only method open to any member of the Church or to any activity or organized grouping of her members is one which serves to realize, in the concrete of actuality, her mysterious action of adaptation.

A particular spiritual danger is that of growing old through a failure to grow up. There are many today who maintain that in the present crisis of unification, through which the world is passing, the Church is dying. Her vitality is ebbing away; her spheres of influence, her prestige, her friendships are diminishing. What she herself calls the "apostasy of the masses" underlines her failure. In previous times she held a monopoly of culture secured by her theology, but now is but a shadow of her former self. Today she is paying the price of an inborn and incurable archaism. She no longer has the ear of men; and all that she retains are the "ruling classes" of yesterday, a liberal economy with which she has become identified and a regime with which she is foundering. Since she is "absent" from the new evolving world, she cannot be counted upon. Against the creative vision of modern humanism, she can offer only a static and theistic world, a philosophy frozen in impossible dogmas, a negative and preconceived system of morality. Christian escapism has taken the virility from the Christian, made him timid in daring, not to be counted upon in conquering the world here below. Man, today, in building his new world expects nothing from the Church; he rejects and thrusts aside her witness from a past age.

To the atheism of aggression, many Christians reply only with a dogmatism of defense.

"There is nothing new under the sun," these say; "it is not the Church which is dead or at fault, but the modern world. Let the storm blow itself out: truth always triumphs in the end. The Church has lived through other crises: she is not afraid of this one. She must refuse to accommodate her message, must remain more adamant than before. The only attitude open to the Church is one of separation. Christianity must return to its traditional forms, invoke those documents which guarantee its rightness. Christians must find their strength in their unity, stand aloof from any form of premature co-operation, and refuse to embody the Church in temporal institutions. She is less afraid of Nero than Constantine."

These rival attitudes in regard to the Church both deny her claims to be an historical reality admitting development and growth, and her deep eschatological sense as the Kingdom of Christ *in via* or on its way. Both notions need to be understood if light is to be thrown on her need to continually adapt herself to contemporary realities.

Regarding the first, Pope Pius XII had something of great importance to give:

While the Church fully asserts her divine origin and super-natural character, she is aware of having come among mankind as an historical fact. Her divine founder, Jesus Christ, is an historical person; his life, death, and resurrection are historical facts. The origins of Christianity and of the Catholic Church are historical facts proved and established in time of space. Of that the Church is well aware. She knows also that her mission, although by its proper nature and aims belonging to the religious and moral spheres and taking place in the life beyond and in eternity, nevertheless reaches into the very heart of human history.[1]

In describing how the Church always and everywhere unceasingly adapts her divine principles of life to a changing and richly variegated human condition, Pius XII describes how she does not function solely as an ideological system.

Undoubtedly she is so defined when use is made of the term *Catholicism*, but this, in her regard, is neither customary nor adequate. She is more than an ideological system. She is a reality like visible nature, like the community of the State. She is a truly living organism with her own end, her own principle of life. Unchangeable in the constitution and structure given her by her divine founder himself, she has gathered up and she gathers up the elements she needs or which she deems useful for her *development of action:* men and human institutions, philosophical and cultural inspirations, political forces and social ideas or institutions, principles and activities.[2]

Implied in such claims is the eschatological character of Christianity and the Church. An apparent loss of this vital dimension accounts (in Père Congar's view) for contemporary unbelief.

[1] Pius XII, Address to the Tenth World Congress of Historical Sciences, English trans. *Catholic Documents*, Vol. 20 (Pontifical Court Club, 1956).
[2] *Ibid.*

At the beginning of modern times [which he posits in the last third of the twelfth century] Christian thought was rather losing sight of the eschatological sense which gives movement and balance to the economy of salvation *in Christo et in Ecclesia.* At the same time, men were beginning to discover history not simply as events in their chronological order, but as a movement toward something: the eighteenth century said toward enlightenment, reason, and progress. By so doing, men were really providing themselves with an eschatology and an equivalent for the Kingdom of Christ. They were giving themselves hope and the equivalent of a religion. But it was a religion of man and a kingdom of the world and of history.[1]

Before one grapples further with the elements of this mystery of adaptation which determines the method to be adopted by the Church in her mission to bring the human person to his full development and maturity, it would be useful to distinguish between two terms which are apt to be confused: technique and method. The Church in this country has seen that, during the last fifty years, more advances have been made in the technique of expression than ever before. As a result, forced by the pace to take advantage of the modern media of expression (press, cinema, radio, and television), Christian teaching and formation have come to rely more on technical skill in presenting its truth than on working out a new and enriched method of harmonizing the supernatural and natural orders in our highly industrialized and scientific society.

Technical skill, however, is no substitute for the more

[1] Yves M.J. Congar, O.P., *Lay People in the Church* (Westminster: The Newman Press, 1957).

profound enterprise of adaptation. When the truth of method is confused with technical skill, there is always the dangerous tendency to oversimplify the problem of human communication. Slickness, the engaging manner, the easy answer, the neatly-rounded truth, the habit of prejudging an issue: all conspire to render negative the essential mystery of Christianity. The communication of divine truth to contemporary humanity loses much of its deep-to-deep call through a lack of care and reverence for the human person whose mind and heart have been fashioned and formed against the background of his own history.

Where the communication of life and truth is concerned, extreme care and delicacy have to be employed. The human person who is the object of the message is not a mass-mind, nor is he a disembodied soul. He exists in time, has an historical background, has been called into existence by God to play a unique rôle in the making of his history. The method, therefore, which the Church adopts to communicate her divine light and life is conditioned by the situation in which the recipient of her gifts exists and by the recipient's exact human condition in time and place.

Much of what we know today about the mystery of adaptation in the life and mission of the Church has been revealed to us in recent years through what has been taking place in her "laboratory" of the foreign mission fields. Here the Church had the advantage of bringing her divine message to peoples who were more "humanly" disposed to receive it. In pagan countries of Africa and Asia she could break free of fetters which, in Europe, had tended to impede her natural development and to conserve her structure at the expense of her inner growth.

Whereas one could identify in European Christianity a certain supernaturalism or attempt in the name of religion to diminish or deny the rôle of nature in the supernatural order, in the mission fields the full impact of the supernatural was possible as the Church first sought out the *originality* and *created* status of what she met in the order of nature, and then effected the mysterious synthesis of the two orders through which a new enriched human condition flowed.

In the mission fields, the Church was able to reveal again something of her rich personality. By examining with clinical precision every human condition, she could uncover the deep affinity of correspondence existing between the authentic expression of "human-ness" and the fullness of her own truth and life. She could bring a unity which transcended all human variety and differentiation, one which, being divine, could not destroy this human variety, but fulfilled it and made it intelligible and meaningful.

True to the first principle of her missionary action—"to understand and to be understood"—the Church, on entering pagan countries, had first to find points of contact at which she could insert her truth of faith into their truths of actuality. Her work was not primarily to build mission stations, erect churches, schools, and hospitals. Wherever she came, she had first to be the pupil, to sit at the feet of the native people, to understand their ways, their wants, their aspirations and hopes, their culture and civilization.

Again it was not merely a matter of knowing their language, of being able to communicate her doctrine in their tongue. She had gradually to take on their mentality, to be incarnated in their culture, to propose Christian truth in their thought forms, to give Christian supernatural life as something which was a complete answer to all their human needs. The Church had to become organically present among these peoples so that she might become their Church.

When Christian missionaries came to Africa, for example, they found an authenic human art which had that universal quality making it a valid interpretation of their way of life. Stunted though it was and lacking a sufficiently spiritual inspiration to bring it to its full perfection, it served the economy by supplying some harmony between man and his environment. Lacking our modern techniques, African native art could still be distinguished by a natural spontaneity absent in modern Western decorative art, with designs which were alive and spiritually moving. It revealed to the African some inkling of the right order of things, suggested the existence of the spiritual order, showed a gleam of the infinite shot into the fabric of human existence on this earth.

The missionary could not ignore this universal value in a pagan people's art, neither could he exploit its racial characteristics at the expense of its underlying "humanness," as was the way of the traders or the commercially-minded. He learned to respect and reverence it as the expression of the life and beliefs of a people, and made it the underpinning of the new Christian order offered to them.

Often, indeed almost always, there was some failure. But native art, in becoming a vehicle for an understanding of super-human truth, was at the same time able to be drawn toward its own perfection without any diminution or impoverishment. From being a mere creative treatment of actuality, it could graduate to its full term as a supernatural treatment of the same actuality in which the people lived its life.

Recognition, therefore, of the *human* value of what is already present in a native way of life is always implicit in the Christian mission to humanity. Christianity is never imposed on an already existing structure of social life. It commends itself to the society which it enters by revealing itself as the full term of all human endeavor and effort. Human life on this earth, in all its rich variegation, finds its true home in the Christian order. In this order it can *truly* be itself, without suffering diminution or loss.

"Listening to the essences of things" is particularly difficult for the Church in the Western world. Western commercial, competitive culture is largely a sham culture. It offers no real interpetation of the meaning of human existence on this earth. Our modern art forms, for example, have as yet been unable to delay the process of modern men's becoming robots in the new age of the machine. They have failed to humanize the effects of an industrialized way of life because they have yet to discover the way to adapt themselves to the new scientific mode of work and to the changed human condition in an industrialized way of life. In place of a social order where its three main elements, work, art, and religion, combine in technique and spirit for the sake of the human person living in society, we now subscribe to the three erroneous formulae of work for work's sake, art for art's sake, and religion for religion's sake.

"Christian art," wrote Abbot Herwegen of the Benedictine Abbey of Maria Laach, "is the art of humanity redeemed." If, then, we wish to see the missionary method of the Church at work again in the norm of parish life, and to lay the first stone of the Christian reality of tomorrow, a deeper degree of recognition needs to be given to the contemporary art forms through which modern industry seeks to humanize the contemporary situation. The mission of the parish can never be content with its organization and ideology. It must seek to become organically present in its local society. To do this, it must first understand what makes the social organism breathe. It must give recognition to whatever is authentically human in those organs of expression through which the social organism seeks the true and the good for its members.

We single out the cinema for examination in this regard for two reasons: firstly, because it is an art form peculiar to modern industrialism; and secondly, because the average Christian reaction to this modern art form gives some measure of the loss we have suffered in understanding the missionary method of the Church.

"To fulfill its apostolic task," wrote Cardinal Suhard, "Christianity needs both a mode of expression and an audience. As a mode of expression, the cinema (as a consequence of its manifold visual and aural possibilities) holds the chief artistic and technical place. It brings into play the whole range of emotional and intellectual activities, and finds a choice field in the realms of science and pedagogy. Its constant evolution enables it to penetrate more and more into the secrets of the human soul—even to abstract reasoning. When one thinks of the road traveled since the beginning and the possibilities open to it (particularly in the use of symbolization), one understands the prodigious future that is before the cinema." [1]

"The film," writes Père Morlion, O.P., of the *Pro Deo* University in Rome, "differs from a series of photographs or paintings, or from a succession of words or musical variations, precisely because each of its constituent elements (shot and rhythm) is chosen simply from its expressiveness in relation to a central theme which is put over to the public. By means of the close-up or pan, of the speech or dialogue, of the musical background, or expressive silence, the film accentuates only that aspect of human reality which inspires the director to communicate that reality as he sees it, to those who will come to his film." [2]

Pope Pius XII, in his constant search to effect a synthesis between eternal and contemporary orders, spoke many times about the intrinsic worth of the modern art form of the cinema. What is particularly evident in his teaching on this matter is the extreme care he had taken to understand its constituent elements. "In truth," he once remarked, "how could an instrument, in itself most noble, but so apt to uplift or degrade men, and so quick to produce good or spread evil, be left completely alone, or made dependent on purely economic interests?"

[1] Emmanuel Celestin Suhard, *International Film Review*, No. 1, 1949.
[2] Felix A. Morlion, O.P., *International Film Review*, No. 2, 1949.

"So far from spending efforts in trying to keep people away from the cinema," said Cardinal Suhard, "let us provide them with a spectacle worthy of their dignity as man. Let us show them, by means of the images on the screen, what might be their lives as children of God, inevitably marked with sufferings, but also joyous and strengthened because based on Him who never deceives. It is necessary that Christians should more and more accustom themselves to judge films at their true value, and that they should use their enormous influence to give the moral and economic support necessary for films of quality. They should not hesitate to call upon the highest artistic and technical ability available whenever they wish to see subjects inspired by religion presented on the screen. They should realize that the most authentic religious film is that which evokes the testimony of a simple life, honest, deeply human, in which every movement is seen to be impregnated with divine love."

Both Pius XII and Cardinal Suhard based their Christian doctrine of the cinema on a precise and scientific evaluation of its natural worth as a human art form. The attitude they adopted toward the film strengthened their hands considerably when they had cause to find fault with the moral content of much that came from the film studios. The film industry was more inclined to take notice of any censures from the Church since they recognized Christianity speaking, not as a religion of morality or chastity, but as a religion of love—love not only for the human person, but for every expression of his human-ness.

Unfortunately the attitude adopted by Pius XII was never fully understood in England where, though Catholic Christians are every bit as regular as their non-Christian neighbors in attending the commercial cinema (nowadays more before their own television screens than in the cinemas themselves), very little if any education has been given for a genuine appreciation of this modern art form.

Not only is this neglect evidence of a spiritual immaturity, it has also perpetrated a great imprudence, for it is not sufficiently realized how the outdated and inadequate practice of confining Catholic film action to a mere moral classification of films has left the door completely open to the far more dangerous effects of the so-called "neutral" film which escapes the censor's strictures.

Today the cinematograph industry offers through these "neutral" films a complete philosophy of life based on half-truths, falsifications of the truth, inanities, and trivialities. In such films the modern onslaught of the superficial on the important finds its greatest ally. "Though morally irreproachable," said Pius XII, "men live and die in these neutral films as though there were no God, no Redemption, no Church. Fed on such a diet, the average cinemagoer becomes incapable of distinguishing good from bad, true from false; his moral faculty expires."

This is not to deny, of course, that the Church has the right and the responsibility of censoring films, but this should not degenerate into a mere press-button mentality, as though once her judgment has been made and propagated about the moral standing of a film that is all that is demanded of the Church. "It is true indeed," said Pius XII, "that the spirit of our times, unreasonably intolerant of the intervention of public authority, would prefer censorship coming directly from the people." Surely if the Church's mission is essentially to form man in his wholeness, an integral part of this mission in every parish is at least to attempt to develop in its subjects a greater spiritual maturity so that the very belief in their own value and destiny would automatically make them more discriminating, selective, and appreciative.

What happens in school and parish leaves much to be desired in this respect. A teacher, concerned with the effect of the cinema on his pupils, will warn the older ones of a certain film, for example, released in the district. Once asking a class of fifteen-year-olds how they reacted to such a warning, the majority quite blandly admitted that it had only whetted their appetites more to see the film in question. In a north country parish where, during a certain week, four cinemas in the town were showing 'X' films, and the fifth a nudist, the action of a Young Christian Workers group in the area was to make representations through their parish priest to the Watch Committee to have the films banned. While in no way finding fault with the solicitude felt by the young people for their comrades' spiritual health, and admitting that such representations have continually to be made, one cannot help thinking that to take such action as the norm of Christian Action and to leave it at that, tends to conceal the deeper work of animation which is at the center of the parish mission. Missionaries in foreign lands continually tell us how important it is, never to take away from the pagan any of his superstitious practices without replacing them with as powerful a Christian equivalent. There seems a lack of purpose in removing a source of entertainment and gratification, however lewd, whatever the success in having certain obscene films banned, without an equal concern being shown for supplying adolescent minds and hearts with a more noble equivalent.

If recognition and ambition is the first principle of missionary action in the parish, the second is that of collaboration. Religion, as mentioned above, is not for its own sake, but for the sake of the human person living in a community, who is the proper origin and end of all social life. It must collaborate with the other elements in the social organism which go to make up its life. The mission of the parish is to form man in his wholeness. The art of the priesthood exercised in the parish through the duality of clergy and laity is a work of reconciliation, of "at-one-ment." This work of reconciliation is not exhausted when the parish reconciles the individual soul to God through its ministry of the sacraments and of the Word. It has also the task of reconciling the whole man in the whole of his cosmic and social situation.

The work of the Church is a supernatural and creative treatment of *actuality*. As a true educator, she does not start from where she thinks people should be, but from where they actually are, i.e., in a form of society largely man-made, and in a world ruled by its own natural laws. Society and the world in which men live were already in existence before the Church. They cannot be bypassed in the life of any parish of the Church. No parish can live its own self-enclosed life as though the society and the world in which it exists were of no consequence.

The mission of the Word-made-flesh was to re-establish

all things in Himself and to restore to all things created their original meaning. For this divine purpose, He incarnated himself in human flesh, in the life of the times when He appeared on this earth, as a member of a human society. Having, with His sacrifice, completed the task given Him by His Father and reconciled humanity, the Father and He sent their Spirit to form the total body of Christ, the Church. Following the law of the Incarnation, the Social Body of Christ incarnates herself in human society and in the life of the times, so that through her members she can apply the "at-one-ment" in time and place to the end of time.

There is first, then, a collaboration between Christ in His Church and the humanity to whom He comes: a mutual give and take, action and reaction, symbolized in the liturgy during the Offertory when to the wine is added a drop of water.

Secondly, there is a collaboration between the Church and those elements in the social organism which go into its make-up and work within it for the sake of the human person, viz., work and art. Human work, like religion, is a law of life and human growth. Art, the crowning glory of technique, likewise plays its organic rôle in the making of man. Religion, work, and art, as essential elements in the social organism all play an organic role and, because of this, all collaborate (or should do so in a healthy social organism) for the sake of the human person. Only in fairly recent times, with the emergence of the modern lay apostolate and the renaissance of the liturgical apostolate, has the full implication of the collaborative rôle Christianity plays in society been recognized. That is why both apostolates need to be seen as something integral to the mission of the contemporary parish.

To search diligently to find the natural affinity or capacity in every created thing, in everything human, for divine grace, the parish must give primacy of place to the organic rôle it carries out in society, and degrade its organized and ideological life from its exclusive sovereignty and "humpty-dumptydom." There are signs, indeed, that its devotion in the past to the formula of religion for religion's sake is slowly being jettisoned.

We hear less talk nowadays about the "dynamite" of Catholic action and less frequently see immature "agitators" for the Catholic cause placing their trust in Catholic blocs or pressure groups. We are growing up as a Catholic community and, with our greater maturity, are beginning to realize that there are no short-cuts toward the Christian reality of tomorrow. Christian action is the action of leaven. It is a slow, developing process. It is a collaborating action, a work of animation.

That there is a long way to go before the average parish becomes aware of its main collaborative organic rôle in local society can be seen by two "witnesses" with totally different reactions to the part work plays in the personal formation of the human being. The first was a remark made by an elderly parish priest to a member of the Young Christian Workers Movement: "Your movement will never catch on in the Church in this country until you take the word 'worker' out of your title." The second was a criticism made by a Catholic working man at the time of a national dock strike:

In the prewar years of depression in my area, when most of us were out of work, the clergy were the Good Samaritans, continually giving us financial and other help when our families were trying to survive on the dole. If only they could realize today that what we want from them is respect. The day of paternalism is gone. Workers like myself want to feel that *as workers* we have something to give to the life of the Church. We want to feel we belong and are needed as workers. Because we are not given this inspiration, most of us in our heart of hearts turn to the Communist Party which in place of the Church in these parts has assumed a monopoly over work and the interests of labor.

"I could not sleep, I was overcome by the revelation it contained," was Cardinal Suhard's reaction in 1943, after spending many hours reading the memorandum on the state of the Christian faith in relation to the proletariat of France, prepared by Abbé Godin. Recently in this country a Trust, set up by the government to study the influences affecting the upbringing of young people today, published, in *Citizens of Tomorrow*, a similar memorandum.[1]

Among its findings, the Trust stressed the fact that in our highly involved and complicated way of life, young people mature much more slowly, mentally and spiritually. A youth today finds it extremely difficult to interpret the complex world he enters after leaving school. To leave

[1] *Citizens of Tomorrow: A Study of the Influences Affecting the Upbringing of Young People* (London: Oldhams Press, 1955).

him isolated in such a situation or reliant on his own "gang" for further formation would be to perpetuate his immaturity. Education, it urged, should go on through all the formative years; indeed, this phase was the most important of all.

The Trust also urged society to pay more care and attention to the great body of young people found between the two extremes of the very bright and the very dull; the modern technological age is making ever-increasing demands on the intelligence of the nation, and educational services must be geared to meet this demand. The untrained "general duty" class of young people should be helped to a higher status in the nation.

A third finding was that there should be a re-examination and eventual reformation of national educational policy and curriculum both as regards school life and the early years at work. Facts showed that there does not exist in this country any real vocational guidance in preparation for working life. Much of the casualness of modern youth could be attributed to the emotional starvation they experienced in their jobs, in the taking up of which they had exercised no real freedom of choice and in which they found few or no opportunities for expansion or growth.

The evidence supplies, we believe, grounds for asserting that the Christian mission to contemporary society is conditioned by the state of that society. For any parish mission to be effective in its work of personal formation and the growth of the human person to full maturity, heed has consequently to be taken of the influences being brought to bear on its people in the larger field of industry, work, and leisure. Its mission must be collaborative with all these influences.

"The Church cannot shut herself up, inactive in the privacy of her churches," declared Pius XII, "and thus neglect the mission entrusted to her by divine providence, the mission to form man in his wholeness and so ceaselessly to collaborate in building the solid basis of society. This mission is of her essence." [1]

[1] Pius XII, Address to the Cardinals, February 26, 1946.

7

Spirituality of the Diocesan Clergy

"*Pascere Ecclesiam Dei.*"
[*To nourish the Church of God*]

"The Christian priesthood is of its very nature a missionary priesthood," said Pope Pius XI in 1936, when addressing the second International Congress of the Missionary Union of the Clergy. The Christian priesthood is the continuation and prolongation of the priesthood of Christ with which it is one in essence, action, and effect. No less than forty times in St. John's Gospel does Christ speak of Himself as the first missionary, "as him whom the Father had sent."

In speaking, therefore, of a spirituality for clergy and laity, fitting them for their complementary functions in the Church, one has always to remember that there can be no Christian sanctity and holiness which is not missionary and does not derive its origin and whole impetus from union with Christ and membership in the missionary

Church. This statement must be taken in both of its two senses, *ex opere operato* and *ex opere operantis*.

In the first place, St. John tells us that as many as receive the Light which is Christ, to them He gives His own divine life, power to live and act as the sons of God. These are born, not of blood, nor of the will of the flesh or of man, but of God. True Christian holiness is nothing less than living and acting on the divine level of existence. It also means that man is reinstated into his original state of justice; he is now as God wills him to be; he is worthy of seeing, knowing, and loving God.

But as we have seen earlier, the three divine energies of faith, hope, and charity are an invitation and call to understand and take part in the activity of God. Christian holiness or sanctity, therefore, includes a willingness on the part of the recipient of the divine life to co-operate or collaborate with God in the fulfillment of his creative and redemptive plans. Of its very nature, Christian spirituality is a missionary spirituality. And since God gives his gifts according to the nature and mode of acceptance of the recipient, Christian spirituality implies a degree of awareness of what one's individual mission in the Church really is, an intelligent collaboration with the designs of God and co-operation in accordance with the needs of the contemporary mission of the Church.

"As Christ assumed a real human nature, so the Church likewise," said Pius XII, "assumes the fullness of all that is authentically human, and by elevating it makes it a source of supernatural power in whatever place and under whatever form she finds it." Christian spirituality, accordingly, is not something uniform: it is Catholic. Men and women of Christian faith are not mass produced. Though all share the holiness of Christ and are branches of the one Vine, the abundance of life they receive from Christ does not destroy or diminish originality or individuation. A spirituality which did not correspond to one's own natural truth, which did not enrich one's own true self, would be a bogus spirituality.

"I am come to make you free," says Christ; free to find one's own truth and complete self-expression, by being drawn into the life and action of God, by taking one's rightful and ordained place in a kingdom where each member is indispensable and makes a contribution all of his own.

"In planning the course of our lives," writes Thomas Merton, "we must remember the importance and dignity of our own freedom." [1] One is nearest to a genuine appreciation of the nature of Christian holiness when it is seen, in its origin and end, in the organic rôle every member of the Church plays in the life and mission of the Church. There can be no genuine spirituality for the human being which does not touch membership of the Church at all points; and since a free and conscious service from the human person whom He has personally created is the will of God, the more freely and consciously a member of the

[1] Thomas Merton, *No Man Is an Island* (New York: Harcourt, Brace and Company, 1955).

Church carries out his individual and unexpendable rôle in her mission, the greater is the degree of conformity with the mind and will of God and of union with Him.

In recent years, much thought and care have been given to present the notion of vocation as something more than a supernatural lottery. Every human person is personally created by God to be a valuable somebody in His divine scheme. It is not sufficient, however, that everyone should have a place in this scheme; it is also important that everyone should be in *his own* place. Essential to a genuine estimation of true Christian holiness is not merely the notion of vocation, but of an *historical* vocation. This is vital since, as Gustave Thibon mentions, man often aspires to become God without actualizing or building up the element in him that is human.

The human body is only spiritually healthy when living his own truth. This truth has many aspects, all of which have to be safeguarded and preserved. A Christian spirituality for woman is particularized by her own femininity, but is also particularized by the exact situation in which woman finds herself in human history and in contemporary society. Modern women need a Christian spirituality developed to the degree of their commitment in the modern world.

"The Mystical Body, like the physical members who compose it," said Pius XII, in 1949, to seminary students, "does not live or move in the abstract outside the ceaselessly changing conditions of time and place; it is always of the century, advances with it day by day, hour by hour, continually adapting its manner and approach to that of the society in the midst of which it must carry on its activity."

The Church of God, the Mystical Body of Christ, is like the men who compose it, a living organism, substantially always the same, but continually, like a living body, growing, developing itself, and tending to maturity. It is in this light one must view Christian spirituality with its source in membership in the Church.

In Christian spirituality, one recognizes an indestructible, unchanging something which is of the order of mystery and the eternal, "a releasing in the creature of the full creative might of God," through which the human being is more deeply plunged into the source of his own natural being. There is a oneness about all Christian spirituality which all share, but it is a divine oneness. It is as far from uniformity and standardization as the infinite is from the finite. Christian spirituality is indeed, from the divine angle, an unvarying constant for all, but from the human it admits of endless variety and change. Changelessness on the divine level is something completely different from changelessness on the human; sameness in the divine idiom, different from that in the human.

For the past twenty years the topic of spirituality for the diocesan clergy has held continual interest, particularly in France. This interest has been revived because it is seen as at the heart of the contemporary mission of the Church. In England, however, the usual reaction has been that such a subject is one not for controversy or even discussion. Spiritual writers and retreat masters in this country are more inclined to maintain that the spirituality of the diocesan clergy does not change and that today it remains the same as it was a thousand years ago. Is their argument so solid as it might first appear?

We can, we think, detect in it a certain illicit transference, which indeed is always present in some degree when Christianity and its spirituality become overrationalized or overregularized at the expense of its essential mystery. By an excessive ratiocination, such spiritual writers oversimplify the treatment of spirituality by naturalizing what is, in essence, supernatural and mystic. They tend to "explain" the divine by evaluating it in terms and measurements merely human. To some extent, they destroy mystery. Christian spirituality thus becomes defined less in terms of an open-ness or response of the human person to all that is implied in a divine creation and more in those of a mold into which people are poured.

Far from being a purely academic question, the matter of a *proper* spirituality for the diocesan clergy has the highest pastoral priority. Today, for instance, we have been told by the Popes that the first task of the diocesan clergy is the personal formation of the laity so that they may take their place in the front ranks of the Church in her contemporary mission. In this formative work, any idea of mass production is designedly excluded. Each individual person has to be formed in his wholeness and in the wholeness of the actuality of his life. The celebration of the Mass, the administration of the sacraments, the preaching of the Word of God, the individual life of prayer of the clergy themselves, are all determined in their nature, pattern, and scope by the aim of the Church which is to bring to fullness of life each organic member of the Church. The *spirit* in which the diocesan clergy enter into their proper task in the Church is something of the greatest importance. For their spirituality to measure up to the demands being made upon them, it is essential that they see it as conditioned by the contemporary mission of the Church. Even the spirituality of the diocesan clergy does not live or move in the abstract outside the ceaselessly changing conditions of time and place.

"Nothing great or living can be done except where men are self-governed and independent," wrote Cardinal Newman; "this is quite consistent with a full maintenance of ecclesiastical supremacy." What Newman was stressing was an essential law of the Church. The service of the community which the diocesan clergy carry out, is eventually to bring each member of the community to his fullness of life in the Church in the full flower of manhood and womanhood. To many clergy at present this appears to be a physically impossible task. How can we, they say, carry out this work of personal formation in a community numbering many hundreds or thousands when perhaps there is only one or two of us attached to the parish?

If we can unearth the roots of this feeling of inadequacy, we should be very near understanding both why so many of the laity are condemned to a spiritual immaturity for the whole of their lives, and why there is a lack of consciousness among the clergy concerning the need for adapting their spirituality to present necessities.

These roots go far back into history, even into pre-Christian history. The great distinction between Christianity and the pagan ancestral religions is that between gospel and myth. Christianity was the first great religion to take this world seriously; it based everything on an intervention of God in human history. Whereas other world religions and many Greek philosophers, Plato particularly, denied the reality or the ultimate importance of this world and posited that of the higher other-world as having the only genuine meaning and reality, the coming into human flesh of the infinite God established the validity of the here-and-now of earthly existence.

"The doctrine of the Immaculate Conception," writes T. S. Gregory, "is a doctrine of the flesh and of history; and those who do not hold it must, at least, appreciate the audacity of poetic imagination which thus laid biological fact where it belongs, in the heart of God who made it. Thereafter the theologian must respect human experience as such and for its own sake.

"For Christmas," he continues, "if it were not incredible, would be intolerable. The Greeks who taught us wisdom turned flesh into word, as Leibniz sought to turn the world into conversation. It is the Almighty whose word became flesh, a human fetus, bathed in the Beatific Vision, an infant who is very God, and *we saw*." [1]

The archetypes behind which the pagan tried to hide from the realism and eventfulness of life on this earth have to some extent been inherited by modern Christians. The philosopher Descartes, in a desperate attempt to reconcile

[1] T. S. Gregory, *The Tablet* (London) Christmas, 1953.

the modern scientific world with the Incarnation, bequeathed to modern clergy the contemporary angelism and supernaturalism which often masquerades under the guise of an incarnational and sacramental Christianity. The spiritual immaturity of the laity is prolonged, not so much because they are neglected by the clergy, their educators in Christ, as because the clergy themselves give insufficient thought to Christianity as a historical reality, and tend to misrepresent the Church as a living organism by overstressing her static organizational and ideological life to the exclusion of the essentially organic mission she must carry out in society. The roots reach back also to the confusion which arose in the early Church between the status of cleric and that of monk. St. Jerome was quite clear about the real distinction: cleric indicated a function, monk a state of life. "The monastic condition has reference to a manner of life," writes Père Congar; "the clerical condition has reference to function, a ministry, a service." [1]

Any authentic Christian spirituality for the diocesan clergy, therefore, cannot be detached from the function they perform in the Christian community. The first and last principle of the sanctification of the diocesan priest is his apostolate. Like the bishop whose assistant he is, the purpose of his life as priest, and his mission in the Church, is to serve a Christian community. By imitating what he does, he sanctifies himself. He becomes another Christ by entering the mission of Christ. "As the Father has sent me I also send you." "Christ who has come not to be served

[1] Yves M.J. Congar, O.P., *Lay People in the Church* (Westminster: The Newman Press, 1957).

but to serve." "Feed my lambs, feed my sheep." "Ordained for men in the things which appertain to God." Such texts as these, which Pius XII uses in *Menti Nostrae* (an allocution to the Catholic clergy) serve to show the intimacy existing between the normal run of parish life and the interior spiritual life of the diocesan clergy.

That this intimacy is sometimes lost sight of, and that the clergy do not always advert to the fact that in the multifarious activities which make up the parish apostolate lies the main source of their holiness, accounts for the tendency to offer the laity a spirituality which does not find its main nourishment in carrying out the duties of *their* own state of life in the actuality of their own earthly existence.

For the laity, individual sanctity and salvation have come to have more meaning than the fulfilling of an organic rôle in the life and mission of the Church. At its peak this individual sanctity resolves itself into devotionalism, the pedantry of piety, and self-righteousness; at its nadir, into a mere observance of rules and regulations.

"Animated as we are," wrote St. Pius X in 1903, in what has been described as the most important sentence of our century, "to see the true Christian spirit once again in every way reawaken and grow strong among all the faithful, the first thing to which we must attend is the holiness and dignity of the Temple in which our people assemble for the one purpose of acquiring that spirit from its first and indispensable source, namely, their own active participation in the Sacred Mysteries and in the solemn public prayer of the Church." [1]

[1] Pius X, *Motu Proprio on Sacred Music*, November 22, 1903.

With these words was inaugurated the modern double lay-liturgical movement to reinvest the faithful with their title of the holy people of God "so that they might worthily proclaim the exploits of God who called them out of darkness into His wonderful light."

It can be readily understood that the service which the diocesan clergy give to the community can never remain a constant. It admits of continual development and growth. As the apostolate of the laity deepens and grows, so, too, does the mission of the clergy. And since from the clergy's mission devolves their spirituality, one can expect a continual adaptation of that spirituality to the changing spiritual needs of the people. Contrasted with the rôle they played in the community a century ago, their service today cannot be restricted to the task of seeing that their parishioners merely keep the regulation of the Church or maintain their juridical identity as her members. Now it is to ensure that, through the normal process of maturation, they fulfill themselves as living stones of the Temple. Like all educators, they need to recognize the original elements in each, to reverence every individual as someone unique in himself, to help each to fulfill the divine ambition infused into each at birth and baptism. If they are successful in this work, they will succeed in giving them a spirituality which is genuinely Catholic, i.e., missionary and organic. In the process their own priestly spirituality becomes also less individualistic and more Catholic.

There were, of course, saints among the diocesan clergy in the nineteenth century in England, but for a priest to live a life of holiness today, his pastoral charity has to seek with scientific precision the authentic human and spiritual needs of the people. He cannot, in fact, apply his charity without taking cognizance of these real, contemporary needs. Divine charity needs always to be applied with the greatest delicacy and care. In our times this care has to be scientific.

"In the matter of charity," writes Père Daniélou, "it will be observed that in monasteries the chief thing insisted upon is that the monk should neither judge nor interpret; with the same meekness and forbearance he must put up with everything that comes his way, ignoring all natural antipathies and sympathies. The apostle, on the other hand, has the duty of judging and criticizing all whom he has to train and guide; he must take his stand on the firm ground of truth, for no solid achievement is ever possible otherwise." [1]

A few examples of where development in the exercise of charity breaks away from established custom may help to clarify the thesis. It may have been the custom to supply the young girls in a parish with the spirituality they needed, by way of the Children of Mary. Devotions to our Lady, sermons on her virtues, processions in honor of her divine maternity, all contribute to developing the ideals of true Christian womanhood, but it is questionable whether today such means are adequate. The greatest tribute to our Lady in modern times comes from those who take their womanhood seriously, seek diligently and with some science to find the obstacles present in contemporary society impeding its full maturation, and aspire to integrating it into the full life of the Social Body of Christ, particularly in times when

[1] Jean Daniélou, S.J., *Action et Inspiration* (Paris: 1938).

an industrialized urbanized way of life calls for the softening and civilizing influence of a truly feminine and Christian witness.

Pastoral charity demands this personal formation in the lives of those who form the parish community. We speak of community as though people today still lived in community, yet we still have to find the new, enriched form of community life which will measure up to the disintegrating influences present in modern life. Here again is a vital work for pastoral charity. It can never presume that the situation is other than it really is. "The first thing required of the active man is that he has some knowledge of reality, namely a directive knowledge, a knowledge referable to action." Charity must go beyond a mere "helping hand"; it must serve to animate, bring its object to an awareness of the creative possibilities at hand in any given situation, encourage the people involved to find their own self-fulfillment in replying to the changes of their times. Almost any aspect of the pastoral mission could be singled out for examination and the conclusion drawn that the revolution called for in its exercise relates not primarily to structure but to development. In fact, any revolution in a parish concerns very little what a priest does, but the level at which he does it.

Every diocesan priest works within certain limitations. He is under a bishop's authority, a member of a diocesan community, charged with a specially visible function, which is multifarious in character, in a definitely prescribed area.[1] These limitations characterize the apostolic function

[1] Gustav Thils, *The Clergy Review* (London) April, 1949.

of the diocesan priest; he works within them and through them. His apostolate bears fruit, not in spite of these limitations, but because of them. Like every art, that of priesthood must know and respond to the natural limitations of the medium in which he works.

Were we to examine each of the different elements in this medium, and assess the effect each has on the spirituality of the diocesan clergy, we might be surprised to find that, instead of nourishing his spiritual life, these characteristics of the diocesan apostolate often hamper its full development. There is the classic example of the saintly Curé d'Ars who even went so far as running away from his parish commitments in order, as he thought, to save his soul.

Bishops are extremely careful to preserve the good will of their clergy, and some go to extreme lengths to avoid bad feeling and antagonism. One wonders, though, how many of the diocesan clergy find a source of spiritual enrichment in their status as his assistants.

"The spiritual progress of Christianity in a diocese, with all its miscellaneous assortment of works and undertakings," writes Canon Thils, "cannot be assured of success without some unifying principle, a central force of attraction, an uninterrupted source of energy and drive, a guarantee of orthodoxy and a vigilant instrument of control: in short, an authority. By divine institution this sacred charge is entrusted to the bishop." [1]

Were a diocesan priest to see more deeply into this element of his own diocesan apostolate, regard the bishop's authority as something "living" or organic rather than "official," and sometimes realize a little more his own obligation and right

[1] *Ibid.*

to keep the bishop better informed about the situation in the diocese, it is fair to claim that he might find, in a sense of "companionship" and collaboration with the bishop, similar spiritual strength to that which he feels when thinking of Christ by his side. We give this as an example of how authority, which in the past was seen as something imposed, could mature into something commended. No priest resents the authority of God or Christ in his life. Why, therefore, when this same authority is vested in a specially chosen human being should it not be a source of spiritual uplift? Perhaps part of the future diocesan revolution will be when bishops take courses similar to those given to industrial management, in order best to commend their authority to those who assist them in the diocesan apostolate.

The diocesan community does not play as great a part as it could in a priest's spiritual life. The more the highly variegated endeavors of a diocese converged toward a central purpose and apostolic objective, the less isolated would the diocesan priest feel in his particular work. How many young priests, for example, lose their initial fervor through this isolation and feeling that they are ploughing a long furrow? How many fall by the wayside because they have been deprived of the friendship and apostolic assistance of their brother priests in the diocesan field? Secular institutes for the clergy and such priest teams which exist in the Y.C.W. movement are sources of spiritual and apostolic inspiration for many of the clergy.

The specially visible function of the diocesan clergy's apostolate also has creative possibilities. No priest need

hanker for the haven of a monastery when he finds so
many opportunities in the parish and diocese for personal
contact with others. Contemplative monks and nuns may
carry out the vital work of long-distance watering of the
soil, but the diocesan clergy work the land. How many
people have been appreciably helped through life by a
kind word or gentlemanly action of a priest on a bus or
train? A sense of being in the world, with the people, and
to some extent sharing at first hand their tensions and strains,
should be a great encouragement to the diocesan clergy
as they follow in the Master's footsteps.

A young priest may be moved overnight from one parish
to another, from a type of work in which he feels at home
to another which fills him with dismay—from comparative
luxury to dismal poverty. Unless he sees the multifarious
tasks in parish or diocese as all for the benefit of the diocesan
community in some form or another, he can so easily feel
self-pity and a resentment at being so placed. If, on the
other hand, he sees in them a source of deeper commitment,
and welcomes the opportunity to learn new competences,
his own apostolic sanctity is enriched and developed. So
very often, however, a priest's seminary training does not
supply him with the ability to adapt established institutions
and practices to contemporary necessities. Many a young
priest, for example, suffers spiritual arrestment by inherit-
ing a youth club when he arrives in a parish and not knowing how to turn it into an instrument of the contemporary
mission of the parish. For years, the club may be his "toy,"
giving him a specious sense of authority and possession.
By the time he learns to discard it, the opportunity of

discovering the true worth of the laity has been lost.

Local residence as a distinctive characteristic of the diocesan clergy perhaps offers most to his spiritual life by reason of the sense of solidarity it offers with people in a prescribed area. Today, however, the diocesan priest cannot hope to preserve for himself the spiritual support he enjoyed until comparatively recently. He has to re-earn it by giving the people a service more in keeping with their present human needs. The paternalism of old is dead, even if unburied. The robust, two-fisted parish priest of the past could only return as a caricature. Nowadays he has to commend his authority to the people by proving that he is contemporary, respects and reverences initiative, healthy originality, and spontaneity, is sympathetic to the lay apostolate, recognizes that he and the people are a duality in the total apostolate of the Church, is not the apostle of conservatism and safety-first. The spiritual fatherhood of the diocesan clergy in its new guise as begetting the modern adult, mature layman and laywoman brings the rich prize of a genuinely missionary and Catholic spirituality.

What we have attempted to do in the previous section is to relate the spirituality of the diocesan clergy to the function they carry out in the apostolate of the diocese. As Canon Masure stresses: the apostolate itself of the diocesan clergy is their first and principal means of sanctification.[1] In their service to the community lies their chief source of holiness.

[1] Eugène Masure, *The Diocesan Priest* (London: Geoffrey Chapman, Ltd., 1957).

For the Church consists of the faithful primarily, the laity, the Christian people. The clergy have no *raison d'être* in the community except to direct it, give it spiritual protection, and keep it in order. The clergy for the people, not the people for the clergy. Apart from the people, the clergy are inconceivable; they are surrounded by the community, formed in it, fed by it. The first and natural state of the Christian is to be a layman; the priest is a layman made a priest. The Christian people is the nourishing soil of the Church. It is to them by definition that everything comes back, and on them everything depends.[1]

For the diocesan clergy, therefore, to serve the community, not only with commitment, but also with proper competence, there must be some acute awareness of the degree and depth of spirituality that people need at any and every stage of their personal growth as members of the Church. This a diocesan priest will never know, unless he becomes fully conscious of the fact that *his spirituality and theirs are but two sides of a common coin.*

The statement of Cardinal Suhard—that there can be no effective clergy without an effective laity—applies also to their respective spiritualities. If the clergy favor a standardized, ready-made, hard-wearing spirituality, conforming to patterns shaped by different generations to meet different needs, the direction and guidance given by them to the laity will tend to root them in the past, not in the present. The responses and replies both give to the inspiration of the Holy Spirit, the soul or *anima* of the Church, will no

[1] Jacques Leclerq, La Vie du Christ dans Son Eglise (Paris: Éditions du Cerf, 1947).

doubt be conscientious, but conscientious in a self-conscious way rather than with a present-day consciousness. "For the Christian soul who weighs history against the mind and spirit of Christ," said Pius XII in a broadcast in 1942, "there can be no question of a return to the past, but only of a desire to go on into the future and to excel oneself."

The clergy cannot give direction to the laity in their spiritual development and growth if they themselves do not know in which direction the whole life and mission of the Church is developing. The whole question of spiritual direction has nowadays to be reviewed. Once it is taken for granted that the type of Christian needed by the world today is one organically present in its life as its animator, spiritual direction can no longer be content with a kind of beauty treatment of the individual soul. The spiritual director today has to give his guidance in the context of the actuality of the life and mission of his client. It can no longer be confined to handing out or applying principles to meet some crisis in a highly individualized form of spirituality. The direction given must be in accord with the objective reality of life in the world and in the mission of the Church in all its contemporaneity. Probably there is no more authentic spiritual director today than the Y.C.W. chaplain who sits patiently on the listening end of a meeting of young people discussing the obstacles they and others like them meet in everyday life, storing up information about the real lives of those he has to form as Christians, and later using the information to insert a little of the truth of faith into the truth of the actuality of their lives, giving them a faith which is interpretative of their actual human conditions and situation, hope to enter into its creative and redemptive possibilities, and love to realize these in the concrete.

One might refer to our times as an age of exchange between the complementary spiritualities of clergy and laity. Each feeds the spirituality of the other. Each prevents the spirituality of the other, becoming a self-interested sanctity. Personal holiness is seen as the holiness of a human person, not in isolation, but in association one with another. To love one's neighbor *as* oneself takes on a new dimension. It is a selfless self-interest. One is not content to love another as much as oneself or even instead of oneself: but simply *as* oneself.

Certain basic requirements can be identified in the spirituality of the diocesan clergy in their contemporary apostolate. First and foremost it is a *prudent* spirituality. "The pre-eminence of prudence," writes Josef Pieper, "means that realization of the good presupposes knowledge of reality." [1] Christian spirituality is not an escapist spirituality. As Father Jungmann expresses it: "The Christian is not meant to be a solitary pilgrim through the darkness of this world, and only in the next to join in for the first time with the songs of praise of the heavenly armies; even here on earth he is to associate with his fellows as the 'holy people of God' and begin to praise his Creator." [2] "Realistic" rather than "practical" spirituality is much more in accord

[1] Josef Pieper, *Prudence* (New York: Pantheon, 1959).
[2] Josef Jungmann, *Public Worship* (Collegeville, Minn.: Liturgical Press, 1957).

with the modern liturgical renaissance, for the earthly liturgy is but the visible manifestation of the activity of Christ in the world. In the liturgy we are invited into an unending celebration. For the Christian every moment of time is worthy of celebration and every day a "feria" or feast day.

A word may be said about Christian detachment. The "nihilism" which so often seems to be an integral part of a certain form of Christian spirituality has no part in the Kingdom of God. If a Christian is encouraged to detach himself from the world, to practice mortification and penance, to undergo *ascesis* or training in the spiritual life, then it is only that he may attach himself more *creatively* to the world in which he lives, to change a former selfish, grasping love of material things and persons for a reverential love of all things created. With his new capacity of seeing things from God's point of view, of "relativizing" them, he sees them as naught only before God, but without doing injustice to their nature.

"Unlike this concept which arises out of growth in love," writes Pieper, "all contempt for the world which springs from man's own judgment and opinions, and not from the supernatural love of God, is simply arrogance, hostile to the nature of being; it is a form of pride in that it refuses to recognize the ordinary obligations which are made visible to man in created things." [1]

The second requirement for the spirituality of the diocesan clergy is that it be universal or truly Catholic. Very often one finds that, whereas parishioners are encouraged

[1] Josef Pieper, *Prudence* (New York: Pantheon, 1959).

to devote their love and interest in the Church to their own parish, they are often deprived of nourishing that love in the rich pastures of the total apostolate of the Church. No parish can survive such treatment, nor can a genuinely Christian spirituality. A universal solicitude or concern is the mark of a mature Christian. Diocesan clergy need always to give a leadership of love in this matter. A narrow parochialism in spirituality can masquerade under many guises. It can show itself in a disregard for the mission of the Church in undeveloped countries, in a lack of sensitiveness to non-Christian thought, in a partisan intolerance and an exclusive interest in spreading the faith in one's own locality by means which smack more of aggression than animation. Every human being, Catholic or otherwise, is worthy of one love only and that is the love of the universal Church.

To animate effectively, such a universal love must be missionary. It must serve to bring about the mysterious synthesis of the divine and the human, the eternal and the temporal, the infinite and the finite. It cannot deface originality, spontaneity, or initiative. Christians sometimes believe that divine charity must needs swamp all natural differentiation. A young girl, for example, will seek to "neutralize" a natural antipathy toward another by covering it over with excessive kindness and generosity, only to find later that she has not resolved the apparent contradiction between loving and liking, and instead of removing tensions and stresses has reinforced them. A good spiritual director will try to show her that human differentiation is the natural underpinning of both hatred and charity. True charity seeks to understand in depth the underlying unity which such differentiation supposes. It discovers that the exercise of the divine gift implies a mutual give and take through which lover and loved both find their true selves and suffer, not impoverishment, but enrichment in their own human differences. Here again, the secret of success is the discovering of one's true self at the actual moment of becoming involved in a communal action which is a sharing in God's own creative and redemptive activity in the world. Not only does God need us; we all need one another if we are to fulfill our organic and indispensable rôle in His plan for mankind.

Thus the third requirement of clerical spirituality is that it become a community spirituality, the spirituality of the Social Body of Christ. No man is an island, but part of the main. "My name is million," wrote a Polish poet, "because I have loved millions and for millions suffer pain." "The servant is not greater than his Master." The clergy have no justification outside the life of the Christian community; the priest offers the sacrifice of the Christian community; he prays the public prayer of the Church; he sacrifices himself for the sake of the Christian flock; for the eternal survival of one sheep in that flock he is ready to suffer martyrdom. He aspires to the highest sanctity that he may the more sanctify others. "If the definition of priest lies in his mediation," writes Cardinal Suhard, "his spirituality—and thus his concrete action in the world—will have to safeguard a twofold series of values: those which make him the man of God and those which really ensure he is the man of men." [1]

[1] Emmanuel Celestin Suhard, *Pastoral Letters*, "The Priest in the Modern World" (London: New Life, 1955).

8

Lay Spirituality

"*Gloria Dei est vivens homo.*"
[*The Glory of God is living man*]
ST. IRENAEUS

Clerical and lay spirituality are, of course, shoots from the one stem of Christian holiness, but each has its own characteristics true to the particular circumstances in which it has to exist. What is particularly interesting about the emergence of a specific lay spirituality in our times is that its clearer definition has helped to throw valuable light on the precise spirituality of the diocesan clergy. This is worth mentioning because growth in the spiritual life has often been impeded in the past for both clergy and laity through a lack of specialization and an aping of one by the other. In the life of the Church, clergy and laity complement one another; so, too, do their distinctive spiritualities.

If one is inclined to doubt the need of a distinctive spirituality for lay folk, it is usually because one has not sufficiently grasped the key position the laity hold in the Church today. At a moment of crisis both for the Church and the world, the layman has become the indispensable missionary who establishes continuous contact between the world and the Church, the temporal and the eternal, the creative and the redemptive work of God. The new type of layman coming into prominence in the Church today is the solution to a dilemma which has dogged the mission of the Church for the past eight centuries.

From the twelfth century on, the Church has been unable to effect a true synthesis of the eternal and the temporal, the contemplative and the practical. We are well aware today of the situation where a new technological world has come into existence without the Church, but it is good to remember that the process started well back in the twelfth century with a rebellion of the priesthoods of second causes against that of the First Cause. Medieval Christendom was undeniably an imposing attempt to actualize a sort of kingdom of God on earth. It approached a maximum domination of the temporal by the spiritual, of nature by grace. Though this alienation was never complete, it sparked off the rebellion of modern laicism and the modern movement to recapture from the Church rights in second causes or in earthly things.

An interesting though unfortunate consequence for the Church was that, in the process of this rebellion, the mystery of Christian faith tended to be sacrificed in the interests of ecclesiastical power. Charles Péguy, in *Clio I*, put his finger on the crux of the matter when he criticized the

French clergy for compromising with the *mystique* (which alone makes Christianity valid) and devoting their energies to propagating a *politique*. "It is one and the same movement," he wrote, "which makes people no longer believe in the Republic and no longer believe in God . . . one and the same sterility withers the city and Christendom." The case of English Catholicism is slightly different, but a like judgment is made by Monsignor Philip Hughes when he attributes the ineffectiveness of the Church's mission to nineteenth-century society to an over-concern for its own interests and a lack of concern for the underlying social ills of the time.

What is so singular about the modern lay movement in the Church is the rediscovery in the new lay spirituality of the element of mystery in normal Christian life. This is one of its main characteristics. To judge its full significance, one needs to examine the credentials of an antecedent spirituality shared often by clergy and laity alike. It has been said that converting worthy people is at times more difficult than saving the infidel. The infidel retains a sense of the mystery in life and subservience to the unseen and invisible, but the average Christian often parts company with genuine religion and the mystery of faith by transferring the center of Christianity from God to himself. The contemporary novelist, Graham Greene, has made various attempts to suggest the particular kind of atheism innate in the pseudo-Christianity practiced by a certain number of its adherents. In *The Quiet American* he seems to get to the root of the matter in a conversation which takes place between the theist Pyle and the agnostic Fowler in a Vietnamese watchtower during wartime:

> Things to me wouldn't make sense without Him.
> They don't make sense to me with Him.

Pyle is typical of the kind of believer who makes God a convenience or utility in his life; he does not accept God on God's terms, but on his own. What matters most to Pyle is Pyle's conscience, which must be safeguarded at any expense, God's or man's. Fowler instinctively reacts against Pyle's impertinence; he professes no belief in God, but has the natural good manners to pay God the compliment of existing on a plane higher than that of the human being; this, once accepted, makes the complete rationalization of human affairs impossible. This sensitiveness of Fowler stands him in good stead at an earlier incident where Pyle refuses to touch the ritual lunch in the Caodist temple for hygienic reasons and cannot understand why his Vit-Health sandwich is refused by the Caodist commandant for religion.

The new type of layman now being formed in the Church for the needs of our age is a much more mature Christian. His adult Christianity is not something stereotyped and mass produced, but of free and conscious choice. He is not content with merely carrying out certain regulations—keeping on the right side of the law—implicit in his juridical membership in the Church. On the contrary, he feels that, as a consecrated layman, he is part of the constitution of the Social Body of Christ and has a constituent part to play in her organic rôle in contemporary society.

For him the Church is a divine mystery carrying out a mysterious action in the world and more than an organization or an ideology.

The modern apostolic layman does not regard his apostolate as something added on to his Christianity, but as a logical consequence of his membership in the Church. Through baptism and the life of the sacraments he believes that he now lives on the divine level of existence and is able to enter God's plan for mankind and play a part in its fulfillment. Christianity for him is the interaction of two loves and two freedoms, the alliance of two persons, God and himself. He reacts to the fact that God proves His respect for the creature He has made to His own image in inviting the human person to act on his level by accepting the invitation on God's terms, not on his own. He is, in fact, irreplaceable in God's scheme of things, and his contribution is something quite unique.

What has brought him to this awareness is his sense of the value of the temporal. The former spirituality of the laity tended to flow from a withdrawal from the world; a modern layman's spirituality flowers in meeting the challenge presented to Christianity by the modern world. Instead of regarding his time on earth as a filling in of time before he reaches heaven, he recognizes that he is providentially put on the earth at a certain time and in a certain place to fill time with God and eternity. His Christianity is essentially worldly in the sense used by Cardinal Newman (for which he was strongly criticized at the time). He is conscious of the fact that "the seventh day of creation marks both the day of rest from the creative work of God and the divine call to man to perfect it," and "that creatures are the path along which man discovers and reaches divine power, high wisdom, and primeval love."

It is important to see that his attitude to the temporal characterizes the spirituality of the layman today. One cannot speak of the complementariness of the clergy and the laity in the Church, necessary for her mission to become effective, if a distinction is not made between their respective rights and responsibilities. The layman in the Church is responsible for bringing the temporal order to the Church. His spirituality, therefore, must be rooted in the temporal just as he himself in his everyday affairs is rooted in it. If it is not so rooted, then his spirituality will fail to interpret or bring a divine meaning to the situation in which he has been placed by Providence; the contribution he makes to the making of God's kingdom on earth will not be his own. The mission of the Church will be hampered by the presence within her of clericalized laymen and laicized clergy.

One of the very interesting points about this "worldly" Christianity is that it re-established contact with the original doctrine about the meaning of human work or co-partnership with the Divine Worker. In so far as the modern layman recognizes a divine significance in whatever he does to perfect creation, he immediately escapes from the unchristian and inhuman formula of "work for work's sake" which is the underlying inspiration of the modern world, and begins to understand the import of God's message to him: "Have leisure and know that I am God."

The importance of a rediscovery of the spirit of leisure

cannot be overemphasized in our day. It is the under-pinning of the whole Christian way of life, especially when the contemporary mode of work—scientific produc-tion—is forcing moralists to review in depth Christian teaching on the Third Commandment and the nature of servile work. Josef Pieper, the German Thomist, has shown that in the emerging world of total work, where the human person becomes less of a person and more of a cog, the higher he rises in the hierarchy of production, leisure has wrongly taken a position subservient to work. On the contrary, as Aristotle maintained, man works only to have leisure. Leisure is not the inevitable result of external fac-tors, of spare time, a holiday, a weekend off, or a vacation. It is, in the first place, an attitude of mind, a condition of the soul, a capacity for steeping oneself in the whole of creation.

The point and the justification of leisure [writes Professor Pieper] are not that the functionary should function faultlessly and without a breakdown, but that the functionary should continue to be a man—and that means that he should not be wholly absorbed in the clear-cut *milieu* of his strictly-limited function; the point is also that he should continue to be capable of seeing life as a whole and the world as a whole, that he should fulfill himself and come to the full possession of his faculties, face to face with being as a whole.

A full spiritual life is denied many today because often human activities are spuriously christianized by throwing a cloak over perverted natural activities. Many of these perversities entered Christianity at the time of Enlightened

Liberalism, when the Church, through an inability to adapt her divine principle of life to a changing human condition, unwittingly through her members adopted the attitudes of the day. One need only mention how generally the organization of the Church has come to mean more for Christians than her organic life; how the essence of virtue is considered to consist in the difficult rather than the good; how the commercial, competitive, "self" virtues stand in lieu of the gifts of the Holy Spirit; how the administration of a parish sometimes is looked upon as more important than the priestly office of mediation. All these are symptoms of a lack of the desiderated contemplative habit, vital for the Christian *mystique*, which can only be put right with a re-discovery of the spirit of leisure.

The spirituality of the modern layman puts him on top of the world as a human being *capax universi* and enables his natural soul to breathe, whereas before it was stifled with a religion reduced to a system. But as he mounts higher, his new vision obliterates only human deformations, not the distinctive features of human variety and differentiation. A second characteristic of his adult Christianity is its social consciousness, its universal friendship, its catholicity.

In his spirituality is a reflection of the anxieties, troubles, and hopes of the Church and the world. He has developed one of the chief elements in Christian adulthood, a universal solicitude or concern. His thoughts, aims, and ambitions have become as wide-embracing as those of the First Apostle. His action as a member of the Church becomes determined in its scope and pattern by hers. His is a missionary spirituality.

But because he is a man of his age, he will use a science of faith to probe and discover the precise human needs and problems which call for a Christian solution. He is not content with a mere organizational or ideological catholicity; for him it must be organic. He knows that the refusal to accept Christianity by so many of his contemporaries is due to the feeling that it does not accept the whole of human nature. People are afraid of being coerced into the Church. Authentic sanctity is seldom presented as bound up with an authentic human life, with the uniqueness, the limited talents and potentialities of the human individual. The belief that the essence of the Church's mission is to form man in his wholeness has too few witnesses and, owing to an overemphasis on the structure of the Church, her development through the rich variety of her members' contributions is omitted from the picture.

The layman is conscious of the vitality and fertility of the Church and sees her catholicity, not merely in terms of quantitative expansion, but as a quality of her being and the capacity of her principle of unity to assimilate, raise up, and restore into the already existing transcendent unity of God every human person and every human value and expression.

This sense of qualitative catholicity is at the missionary layman's hand, because, being in the front ranks of the Church, he strives to make the Church the vital animating principle of unity in contemporary society. He reaches such spiritual maturity through his concern for the temporal. He sees a new world coming into existence without the guidance and help of the Church. Since he is both a member of the Church and a citizen of the world, he recognizes that he has a double vocation as a member of each. God is calling him to holiness through profane activities. His task is to restore a divine meaning to human effort, to make human progress intelligible, to effect a synthesis between the divine and human, the supernatural and the natural, the eternal and the temporal.

It is not unknown for a priest engaged in the pastoral apostolate to feel that his multifarious activities in the service of the community hamper his individual sanctity. Only a constant reminder that his service to the community is the main source of his sanctification helps him to resolve his dilemma. The same problem faces the modern layman in the Church. The urge is to keep in watertight compartments his commitment in the world and his individual spiritual life. The layman, too, finds the solution to his difficulties in the reminder that his spirituality is fettered to his membership in the Christian community. This love of the community is the third characteristic of his spirituality.

The effects of modern industrialism and urbanization on human family, personal, and social life have yet to be fully gauged, but we know enough about them to recognize that in their train follow social disintegration and the atomization of the family. As Christians, we still talk rather glibly about the family being the bedrock of civilized living and the main educational influence in society, unaware at times that, with any great change in the social organism, the family and the community need both to adapt and enrich themselves to face up to the new and greater demands made upon them.

In our own times we notice that many institutions arising from the natural law no longer completely fulfill their task. Contemporary social life continuously grows more complex with an ever-growing variety of human relationships: members of the one family working in different places and at different jobs, continuously widening their interests and seeking new fields for their abilities, sharing their loyalty to the family circle with organizations and societies necessary for the upholding of their human or professional rights. We live in a plural society. Life outside the home assumes a multiplicity of aspects, all of which can enrich family life but very often, because of a lack of awareness of their full effect on personal life, serve to break up into various facets the impact of evil.

The situation in which many today live their lives is a highly-involved and confusing one. We have, as yet, failed to gauge the precise effects of modern industrialized, urbanized life on personal and social life. Part of the mission of the Church is to bring to the surface and to define the present questioning of modern man about his civilization. Part of the Christian reply to the modern dilemma is to help people to perceive the questions or to ask the right questions. There are as many solutions proffered as there are ideologies, and very often the Christian solution suggested is merely on the surface and ineffective because it has failed to dig deep enough to reach root problems.

Only the layman who is present in the world as its citizen and involved in its construction can throw sufficient light on the subject. With the sense of human solidarity which is innate in his spirituality he is able to recognize in depth the pressures causing spiritual and social disintegration. At a moment when the Church enters her third great missionary era and strives to bring temporal realities into her life and the light of the Gospel to the structures of modern society, the layman is irreplaceable as her eyes and her ears.

In our century the mystery of brotherly love in the community of the Church is acquiring the same community spirit as that of the first centuries. This spirit is being vocalized in the liturgy, and a community of action is flowing from a community of prayer.

After the Bible, wrote Cardinal Mercier, the most important subject for the priest is society. His words have an added urgency today. Contemporary society appears to be developing to the full, as a kind of universal humanism, without the inspiration and guidance of the Church. The layman in the Church has become her indispensable missionary, establishing continuous contact between her and the world. As yet, there are too few laymen who are being brought to their full development as adult members of the Church. Without them she cannot carry out her mission of unification in a world growing to adulthood. The main task of the clergy today, as Pius XII never failed to repeat, is the spiritual formation of the laity. They are in the front ranks of the Church, and without them she can neither establish contact with contemporary society nor collaborate with the new science of work and the new science of art which are its basic elements. But they need the spirituality measuring up to their double vocation as organic members of the Church and citizens of the world. It is a spirituality which does not take them out of the world, but one which enables them to interpret it, a "worldly" spirituality, a sacramental one, one bringing with it a sense of the Church and a deep sense of human solidarity.

Index